Nuffield College Studies in Economic History

No. 1 : The Industrial Revolution

Nuffield College Studies in Economic History

THE
INDUSTRIAL
REVOLUTION

Edited by

R. M. HARTWELL

BASIL BLACKWELL
OXFORD
1970

ISBN 0 631 12500 0

Library of Congress Catalog Card No.
71–120938

Printed in Great Britain by
BURGESS AND SON (ABINGDON) LTD ABINGDON BERKSHIRE
and bound by KEMP HALL BINDERY OXFORD

Contents

Introduction

This is the first of a series of studies in economic and social history by members, and ex-members, of Nuffield College, Oxford. This series, which will not appear regularly, but will match the ingenuity and productivity of the College, reflects the strong interest in the College since its foundation in the economic and social history of modern Britain. G. D. H. Cole was an early fellow, and the College was very fortunate in acquiring his library as the basis of a now much larger research collection in the economic and social history of Britain of the last two centuries. Beginning with G. D. H. Cole the College has usually had one or more economic and social historians among its fellows, including K. H. Connell, P. G. M. Dickson, J. F. Wright, E. L. Jones, B. H. Harrison, and G. Stedman-Jones. The College has also had a number of prominent overseas economic historians as visitors: J. R. T. Hughes, L. Davis, C. P. Kindleberger, A. R. Hall and S. Engerman. Since 1956 the Reader in Recent Social and Economic History of the University has been a professional fellow of the College, and, strategically, its Fellow Librarian. Since the mid-fifties, also, there has been each year in the College a small group of students of social and economic history, most of whom are now university teachers both in Britain and overseas. The bias of studies of these students has been, and is, modern, and there has been, in particular, an abiding interest in the English industrial revolution. This has meant that there has been continuously in the College a formal or informal seminar group, with no particular ethos but with a common interest in the socio-economic problems of industrial Britain. This interest, and the consequent research and discussion, has led to many theses, and many publications. Much of value, however, has been left unwritten or lies buried in unpublished theses and papers. The following selection of essays, concentrated on the industrial revolution, makes available some of this unpublished material, and demonstrates certain themes which have motivated Nuffield College studies. Other selections, with different themes and different time periods, will follow.

This selection of essays on the industrial revolution is divided into two sections—on economic and on social history—and ranges from discussion of the origins of the industrial revolution (E. L. Jones) to its social consequences (R. M. Hartwell), from modern themes in the economics of growth (N. von Tunzelmann) to traditional themes in social history (M. E. Rose), from methodology (P. E. Razzell and D.Whitehead) to the novel theme of the economics of religion (C. M. Elliott). The essays demonstrate, collectively, the richness of sources and themes on industrial revolution studies which still remain relatively unexplored, the value of more detailed research on already well-explored themes, the need for a more careful methodology of economic and social history, and the great and increasing value of economic and social theory as the essential tools of research for the economic and social historian. Indeed, much of this volume is *new* economic and *new* social history. Much has now been written about 'the new economic history', especially in the United States of America, but practically nothing has been written about 'the new social history'. New economic history, *Cliometrics* as the Purdue school entitled the subject matter of their famous yearly meetings, has revolutionized the study of economic history in America. Sadly the systematic and advanced teaching of its essential tools (economic theory, econometrics and statistical theory) is rarely found in departments of economic history in Britain. The new economic history consists of the proper training of economic historians as economists, and of the most rigorous use of theory and statistics in the writing of economic history. In varying degrees all the economic essays here are essays in new economic history, but particularly those of D. Whitehead and N. von Tunzelmann prove that economic theory is necessary to do certain things in economic history. New economic history in Britain has often been written by economists (A. K. Cairncross, B. Thomas, A. Lewis, E. H. Phelps-Brown, for example) but rarely by economic historians (H. J. Habakkuk and P. Deane being honourable exceptions). Indeed until departments of economic history make it possible for at least some economic historians to train as economists, the profession of economic history in this country will remain backward compared with America where economic historians (for example, R. Fogel, L. Davis, D. North, R. Gallman, R. Easterlin, P. Temin, P. David, A. Fishlow, etc.)

are producing such novel and exciting new work. Comparable work in Britain is being done only by a handful of younger historians and economists, in contrast to the increasing number of young Americans who see clearly the potentialities of the massive sources available in Britain for the analytically minded economic historian.

In contrast the new social history in Britain flourishes. For this there are two main reasons. The first is a strong and abiding interest in social problems which dates back to the industrial revolution, an interest prompted in the first place by the social ills of an industrializing society. This interest has been coupled usually with a radicalism which has continuously criticized both contemporary conditions, and also historians' interpretation of past conditions. This challenge has resulted in excitement and controversy, and has stimulated a large literature. The radical social historians, like the Hammonds and R. H. Tawney, have had considerable influence, both from their social criticism and from their history. To the extent that this social history is long-standing, it is, of course, not new; and there is little distinctive in the way of method in the social history now being written, certainly nothing as novel as the analytical and quantitative methods of the new economic historians. The new social history can be viewed rather as a radical change in interest and effort than as a radical change in method. Social history, although always important, now represents a major intellectual input in Britain; it attracts an increasing number of good graduate students; some of the most important publications in history come from the pens of social historians. The second reason for the new social history, therefore, is a fundamental change in the interest of historians away from political and constitutional history, towards social themes; this change in interest is particularly evident among the general historians. Thus the dimensions of historical inquiry have been enlarged, and more historians, proportionately, devote themselves to social history. In particular there is a great interest in class structure, in social classes, in class conflict, in class culture; there is a fascination with the irrational and the bizarre in history; there is great effort to link culture, economy, and society; there is renewed interest in education and religion. Thus essays on the history of witchcraft, mob violence, popular culture, *omerta*, sex, the status of women, milennial movements, revolutionary plots, etc., are piling up, adding to our knowledge but as yet not greatly to our understanding of modern history. But, whatever the results, there is no doubt about the movement, a fundamental shift in interest and effort towards social history. In this volume, the essays of P. E. Razzell and C. M. Elliott represent such a change in interest.

No neat conclusions of a general nature can be drawn from the essays in this volume; nor was it intended, in the planning of this particular volume, or of the series, to do so. The aim, in writing this Introduction, was not to draw conclusions about the industrial revolution but rather to point out some trends in British historical scholarship. Nuffield College, while not necessarily typical, does represent one type of training for the social and economic historian, the results of which can be judged from these essays.

R. M. HARTWELL
Avalon (Australia)
19th August, 1969.

A

Essays in Economic History

1

D. WHITEHEAD

The English Industrial Revolution as an Example of Growth

I

Not for the first time a reappraisal of the English industrial revolution is taking place. A change in the aims and methods of economic historians has been visible for at least a decade and with the publication of Deane and Cole's study of *British Economic Growth*[1] there is now a major work exemplifying the new approach. The stimulus for the present revision has come as an offshoot of interest in contemporary economic development and it has two objectives. As an historical exercise it is designed to provide a more precise account of the timing, pace and causes of this first example of sustained economic growth. As an adjunct to the study of the problems of underdeveloped countries it is intended to offer a guide to policy:

'Clearly, the character of the initial acceleration and its preconditions are of particular interest, not only to those who are seeking an explanation for the first industrial revolution, but also to those who are concerned with policies which may launch modern pre-industrial economies into a path of sustained growth.'[2]

The new approach has not—*mirabile dictu*—been ushered in by a denunciation of the old but the reasons for dissatisfaction with the previous treatment of the subject are clearly implied by the form the revision has taken. At root the cause of discontent with traditional accounts of the industrial revolution is that in comparison with studies of underdeveloped countries they seem vague about its causes and, indeed, about the appropriate use of that shapeless historians' net the concept 'industrial revolution' itself.

[1] Phyllis Deane and W. A. Cole, *British Economic Growth 1688–1959: Trends and Structure* (Cambridge, 1962).
[2] Ibid., p. 278.

As Hartwell recently wrote: 'On the origins of the industrial revolution, the historians have been neither very illuminating nor particularly argumentative, being seemingly happy to accept simultaneously a number of suggested solutions without testing their mutual consistency, either deductively or empirically'.[1]

At first sight this criticism may seem surprising. Writers such as Ashton and Mantoux give every impression of presenting their accounts of the industrial revolution as an intricate but linked causal chain. In large part the apparent analytical strength of such studies is derived from an explicit and implicit framework of interlocking economic and social theory. However, this framework itself needs close examination since it is here that the contrast between the old and the new can be most easily seen. Understandably the chief contribution to the framework has been made by economists. Ever since Adam Smith showed how the wealth of nations increased through the interaction of division of labour and the extent of the market economists have traced more and more elaborate self-reinforcing growth sequences. As a result of their labours the historian of the industrial revolution now has at hand a set of models that show how sustained growth can arise from the feedback between such familiar elements in history as increased investment, larger scale and more specialized production, technical change, sharpened appetites for goods and more responsive factor supplies. Beyond these narrowly economic sequences the historian is heir—sometimes unwillingly—to those themes and their numberless variations which have sought to show how a growing economy influences society in ways that sustain growth. The spinning of the materialist web has been carefully observed; the shift in the balance of power to the prospering commercial and industrial groups; decay in respect for traditional wisdom and values as they become inappropriate; the rise of business centres encouraging new attitudes and ideologies; acquisitiveness with its penumbra of thrift and industry enthroned as the source of general welfare.

These are the props that support traditional narratives of the industrial revolution, but the implication of recent work is that they are inappropriate for this purpose. Essentially this is because such a theoretical framework offers no analysis of the transition

[1] R. M. Hartwell, 'The causes of the Industrial Revolution. An Essay in Methodology', *Econ. Hist. Rev.* 2nd series, XVIII (1965), p. 165.

to sustained growth: explanations are provided for the ongoing character of growth after it has been set in motion but not of why it begins. Indeed, without excessive caricature, the theories can be seen simply as elaborations of the proposition that economic growth is its own best lubricant. It would clearly miss the point to reply that the actual initiation of growth is a trivial problem; that any of a myriad of exogenous shocks could have been the *primum mobile.* In terms of the 'take-off' or 'turning point' hypotheses the critical problem within the conventional framework is not to explain why growth occurred but why its occurrence was delayed; if the forward movement of the economy is so irresistible why nevertheless, it was so long held in check. In this context the plethora of favourable shocks to which the economy was doubtless subject in the course of centuries becomes an embarrassment. The gravamen of the charge against traditional accounts of the industrial revolution is that they obscure its most important characteristic: that it marked a fundamental discontinuity in the growth pattern.

The approach of recent writers to the task of 'explaining' the industrial revolution has involved three preliminary steps. First, the system of national income accounting is employed as a conceptual and statistical framework of analysis; with its help the available quantitative information is assembled so as to gauge as accurately as possible the size and structure of output in the economy and their change through time. Second, using the measures of the economy that have been derived in this way, attention is focused on the overall rate of economic growth. Third, by examining the rate of economic growth an attempt is made to locate a 'fundamental turning point' in economic development, that is a point—or more than one point—of inflection in the growth path where the rate of growth suddenly and 'permanently' accelerated. Each of these steps is more precarious than the last. The statistical information from which the basic estimates are constructed is incomplete and unreliable. Consequently the derivation of rates of change is subject to large errors. This is partly because the underlying data is so grossly inaccurate that the extent of the inaccuracy is itself likely to show rather large changes but the more important reason is that the calculation of growth rates greatly exaggerates any change in the accuracy of the underlying data. For example, if 80 units are recorded out of a total of 100 in the first period and 84 from a total of 101 in the second period the small percentage improvement in recording produces a *fivefold* overstatement in the rate of growth. The last step—the identification of turning-points—is still more uncertain: statistically it involves an attempt to identify a change in the rate of change of highly suspect series; conceptually it involves trying to disentangle a 'fundamental' change from among such powerful shortrun influences as war, disease and the seasons.

Clearly the attempt to discover a fundamental turning-point in the growth path of the eighteenth century economy is extremely hazardous. However, if it can be located two advantages seem to follow. First, the crucial historical discontinuity can then be identified with it and thereby precisely defined; in this matter it is of minor importance whether the turning-point is labelled 'industrial revolution' or that term retains its wider and vaguer meaning and a new term such as 'take-off' is coined. Second, the proximate causes of the industrial revolution can be sought by an examination of the economy in the vicinity of the turning-point. The concept of a fundamental turning-point in the process of English economic development provides the major contrast between the new and the old in their approach to the basic task of explanation. Without it the introduction of national income accounting as a statistical and conceptual framework offers a useful and important adjunct to investigation—in many respects a fundamental one—but it provides no dramatic restatement of the problem to be explained and promise of a solution in sight. It is the notion of a turning-point which removes the vagueness of the old approach by precisely defining the phenomenon to be explained; it is the idea of a jump in the rate of growth of total and average income which suggests—as we shall see—the use of a radically different body of economic theory from that underlying traditional accounts. All of this assumes, of course, that the existence of a fundamental turning-point can be taken for granted. Certainly this seems to be the view of Miss Deane in her recent study of *The First Industrial Revolution*:

'Although there is still room for considerable differences of opinion concerning the exact timing of the *crucial* turning-points in British economic development, there is a general consensus among economic historians that sustained growth—modern economic growth some would say—can be traced back to the middle decades of the eighteenth century. Before then economic change was generally slow (when not precipitated by non-economic catastrophes); and standards of living tended to fluctuate violently in the short run and to rise (or decline) imperceptibly in the long run. Afterwards change became continuous, evident and systematic—it was part of an industrialization process which was as apparent to contemporaries as it is to us in retrospect: and national output, population and incomes per head began to grow, at varying rates it is true, but with only short term interruptions. Economic growth—sustained and perceptible—became part of the normal order of things.'[1]

This paper will present a contrary view: that a fundamental turning-point in English eighteenth century development is not merely difficult to identify but that its existence is unlikely.

II

The idea of a fundamental turning-point was first introduced by Professor Rostow in the form of his take-off hypothesis.[2] Rostow argued that the growth path of every economy can be usefully regarded as conforming to a uniform sequence of stages. The keystone of this sequence is the take-off phase: a period of some two decades that marks the transition of each economy from stagnation, or limited spasmodic advance, to modern self-sustained growth. This attempt to produce a systematic and unified account of modern economic history attracted considerable attention; as with Turner's frontier thesis the broad vision, pleasing ideological overtones and effective style of Rostow's work all contributed to the interest with which it was received. However, Rostow's views have been strongly challenged and in the light of the evidence that has been collected so far it seems unlikely that a well-defined take-off phase occurred in the growth path of most already developed economies. Indeed, Rostow himself has restated the take-off hypothesis in a vaguer form which associates the transition with a qualitative change rather than a spurt in the growth of aggregate income.[3] Accordingly, it cannot be assumed

---

[1] Phyllis Deane, *The First Industrial Revolution* (Cambridge, 1965).

[2] W. W. Rostow, 'The Take-off into Self-sustained Growth', *Economic Journal*, LXVI (1956), p. 32, and *The Stages of Economic Growth* (Cambridge, 1960).

[3] W. W. Rostow, 'Introduction and Epilogue', and 'Leading Sectors and the Take-off', in *The Economics of Take-off into Sustained Growth*, ed. W. W. Rostow (1963).

that there is any presumption in favour of a turning-point in England's development based on the general occurrence of this phenomenon; rather the presumption that might be derived from studies of experience elsewhere is in favour of a more protracted transition than the take-off hypothesis envisages. It is curious, therefore, that Deane asserts the existence of a fundamental turning-point so firmly especially since she has been one of Rostow's most forceful critics.[1] True, the take-off hypothesis has been substantially modified in her work with Cole. In one sense the hypothesis has been made much more general since it has been stripped of the two particular characteristics that Rostow held to mark each transition: a rise in the proportion of national income invested and the emergence of one or more dominant industries. In another sense the hypothesis has been made less general since it is no longer held—or at least not explicitly—that every economy experiences a crucial turning-point. Nevertheless, the concept of a fundamental turning-point as it is applied by Deane and Cole to the English economy is clearly derived from the original take-off hypothesis and retains the same essential feature: that transition to self-sustained growth is initiated by a marked and sudden acceleration in the advance of aggregate income. The appeal of the turning-point hypothesis seems to result from an analogy drawn between the spontaneous growth of the English economy and the growth path that may well be created by in-duced development in some—or most—contemporary countries. This analogy is explicitly drawn by Rostow. He does not discuss its validity but within his framework of analysis such a discussion is unnecessary since the justification for the analogy flows from his general argument and evidence in favour of a uniform sequence of stages experienced by every country. However, although Rostow's all-embracing scheme seems to have been rejected the influence of the analogy still seems to persist in recent work without any explicit discussion or attempted justification. Yet, once the analogy is examined, the contrast between spontaneous and induced development seems to considerably weaken the case for applying the turning-point hypothesis to the English situation.

In some backward areas it is probably realistic and helpful to envisage the economy as held in a low level equilibrium trap by a balance of economic forces. Since so many examples of long

[1] H. J. Habakkuk and Phyllis Deane, 'The Take-off in Britain', in Rostow, ibid.

continued stagnation are to be found it seems inherently more likely that in many instances this is because growth itself produces forces that reverse the tendency to expansion rather than that the coefficients of numerous economies happen to have just those values that maintain a long term constancy in income per head.[1] In such a situation when growth begins, or even where efforts are made to secure it, the forces making for growth can be clearly seen: characteristically they are the product of a government plan. For a time stimuli will be applied without obvious effect and this gives content to the notion of preconditioning. But when, and if, escape is made from the trap and average incomes begin to grow, hope—if not analysis—suggests that development will rapidly reach a satisfactory rate. In this situation there is a clearly marked turning-point: the escape from the low level equilibrium trap together with the onset of the growth in average income is both analytically distinct and statistically recordable.

Such a scheme does not seem plausible when it is applied to the evolutionary English situation. Here, where a capitalist, industrial, ultimately science based, engine of economic progress was forged for the first time it seems quite arbitrary to separate off the phase of pre-conditioning from the phase of growth. For the most part the attitudes, institutions and techniques conducive to growth were themselves moulded by economic advance and adopted in response to economic opportunities. The process is one of conditioning by growth—long continued and cumulative even if sometimes reversed—rather than preconditioning. Contemporary underdeveloped areas undergo a revolution in the attitudes, ideologies, industrial techniques and political-industrial-financial-commercial structures they employ but they do not—in general—have to devise as well as introduce these changes. That England had to do so helps to explain why the eighteenth century was marked by intense activity and modest accomplishments. In such an evolutionary situation the interaction between growth accomplished and growth sought seems likely to be a much more complex and protracted process than in most cases of induced growth. In such a situation spurts in economic advance will probably occur. Indeed, they were inevitable—together with subsequent relapses—in a period in which war, disease and the seasons played

[1] Cf. H. Leibenstein, 'Population Growth and the Take-off Hypothesis', in Rostow, ibid., especially p. 172.

upon an uncontrolled economy undergoing a self-devised technical and economic revolution. But in such a sequence it is difficult to ascribe any 'fundamentalness' to such forward movements.

The false analogy between induced and spontaneous development seems to have led to an oversimplified view of the industrial revolution as an historical discontinuity—or of the nature of the discontinuity—and a misplaced emphasis on the identification of the proximate causes of some distinct and limited occurrence. It seems that if the metaphor of a growth curve is required—and simulation of this sort may obscure more than it reveals—the picture of the industrial revolution that is least misleading is probably one of gradual, and often interrupted, acceleration over more than a century. Adopting this view of eighteenth century development deflects the major criticism of traditional accounts of the industrial revolution and their theoretical framework that was set out above. There is no central episode to be identified and explained so that conventional accounts cannot be indicted for omitting it. The origins of English growth were slow, halting and remote, not a sudden leap that has been obscured by an inappropriate pair of theoretical spectacles.

This does not mean, of course, that existing accounts offer a satisfactory explanation of the industrial revolution. Their essential weakness is that they are non-quantitative. As an illustration of this characteristic it is instructive to look at Adam Smith's model of growth through a widening of the market which Professor Habakkuk has called—with justice—the most reasonable explanation of early European development that has yet been provided.[1] In the light of Adam Smith's discussion it is easy to envisage a growth sequence in which an extension of the size of the market is both induced by and in turn induces an increase in the division of labour. But what is left quite unclear is the rate at which growth will take place and whether this rate will be accelerating, constant or slackening. Increasing the complexity of the sequence—for example, by introducing technical change—allows the historian to organize a greater number of factors and therefore tell his story with greater richness and intricacy but it does nothing to overcome its fundamental weakness. Reference to

---

[1] H. J. Habakkuk, 'The Historical Experience on the Basic Conditions of Economic Progress', in *Economic Progress*, ed. L. H. Dupriez (Louvain, 1955), p. 150.

underlying theory of this type is almost akin to a conjuror's wave: it distracts from the inadequacy of the narrative rather than indicating it or still less helping to repair it. Perhaps the plainest indication of the weakness of the explanatory apparatus used in traditional accounts of eighteenth century development is that it is difficult to think of any part of it that would be employed by any economist attempting to forecast the rate of growth of any economy over any time period. In contrast, the strength of current studies is that they have begun to use an analytical framework that is conceptually quantifiable and to accumulate and sift the evidence that might be linked with it. Perhaps by this means it will become possible to unravel—however tentatively—decade by decade the proximate causes of English development so that these in turn may be related to the changing social and economic environment. However, it is argued in this paper that our interim understanding of the processes at work and the long term nature of the task involved in acquiring a better understanding of these processes seem in danger of being obscured by an inappropriate analogy, an inappropriate concept and an inappropriate redefinition of the problem to be explained. So far these criticisms have been made in general terms but in the next section of the paper an attempt will be made to evaluate the evidence for a turning-point in English economic development during the eighteenth century.

III

The case for believing that England's economic development in the eighteenth century was marked by a 'crucial turning-point' would need to be established in two ways: by examining the available indices to see whether they reveal periods in which a pronounced acceleration in growth occurred; and by a rather more general consideration of the structure of the economy to decide whether it seems likely to have produced such discontinuities. Of these two approaches the seemingly more direct method of compiling statistical evidence for the existence of sharp breaks in trend is hazardous because of the paucity and unreliability of the available data; consequently considerable weight must be attached to an assessment of the probable workings of the economy. In addition an attempt to understand the structure and functioning of the economy is necessary in order to explain the turning-point—if any—and thereby to demonstrate in what sense it is 'fundamental'. Both of these approaches were adopted by Deane and Cole in *British Economic Growth*. They concluded—from the extensive data that they had assembled and processed—that, although there was some increase in the rate of growth of the economy towards the end of the century, the first acceleration in output which initiated sustained growth should be placed in the 1740s. This transition was related to the underlying movements in the economy by a mechanism for which they found support in contemporary opinion and, apparently to underline its 'fundamentalness' they contrasted their triggering mechanism with other explanations of eighteenth century growth—such as the expansion of foreign trade—all of which they held to be derivative rather than primary causes of growth. It will be argued that on neither ground—analysis or statistics—have Deane and Cole made out a convincing case. Instead, it will be argued that the evidence accords more closely with a picture of occasionally interrupted but recognizable and cumulative growth reaching back to at least the beginning of the eighteenth century without any obvious 'turning-point' in this development; that, on balance at least, the evidence supports the view of the development sequence that was advanced on general grounds in the first part of this paper. This section of the paper will be concerned almost exclusively with an examination of the thesis advanced by Deane and Cole since they have provided by far the most comprehensive, detailed and formidable support for the turning-point hypothesis. However, by discussing their thesis it is hoped to establish that—in no mere one swallow sense—growth of a recognizably modern sort stretched back to at least the beginning of the eighteenth century. And, that such faltering as there undoubtedly was in the 1740s and 1770s was not the breakdown of an inadequate economic engine but the not surprising accompaniment of unfavourable factors—overwhelmingly, war.

Dean and Cole paint a somewhat gloomy picture of the first part of the eighteenth century and particularly of the period *circa* 1725-45.

'In sum, then, it is probable that most of the rather modest progress made in the first half of the eighteenth century took place in the first twenty to twenty-five years, and that the movement was then checked for about twenty years before the much stronger, many-sided wave of expansion which began in the 1740s and gathered momentum in the ensuing decades.'[1] They trace the check to expansion in the 1730s and 1740s to a shortage of labour and a shortage of demand for manufactures which are alleged to have come about in the following way. In this period agricultural prices were low. The low prices were caused by an increase in agricultural output that was not fully matched by a rise in demand: a succession of favourable seasons occurred at a time when population was almost stationary and—despite an increase in corn exports and the amount of grain distilled for spirits—cereal prices fell both absolutely and in comparison with the prices of manufactured goods. For farmers the fall in prices outweighed the increased volume of output and they suffered a decline in income. Part of this decline was passed on to landlords who permitted rent arrears and assumed a larger share of expenses involved in maintaining and improving their estates. As a result of this decline in income farmers and landlords reduced their demand for manufactured goods. The reduction in demand from this quarter was not offset by increased purchases by labourers—whose real incomes had risen—because this group preferred to take out their extra real income in the form of additional leisure. Hence the shortage of labour as well as of demand. Essentially, the hypothesis advanced by Deane and Cole is that a fall in agricultural prices led to a redistribution of income away from a group with a high marginal propensity to spend—farmers and landlords—to a group with a lower propensity—the labourers.

At first sight this reconstruction follows from a reasonable interpretation of two pieces of evidence. The first of these consists of the numerous indications that the income of farmers was reduced by the price fall and that this reduction was shared, in part, by the landlords: indeed, because of this, the period has been dubbed an 'agricultural depression'.[2] The second consists of the abundantly documented testimony of well-informed contemporaries that there was increased difficulty in obtaining labour when provisions were cheap.[3] However, on closer examination,

[1] Deane and Cole, op. cit. p. 61.
[2] G. E. Mingay, 'The Agricultural Depression, 1730–1750', *Econ. Hist. Rev.* 2nd ser. VIII (1955), pp. 328–38.
[3] The best summary of evidence is in E. Furness, *The Position of the Labourer in a System of Nationalism* (New York, 1920) but see also D. C. Coleman, 'Labour in the English Economy of the Seventeenth Century', *Econ. Hist. Rev.* 2nd ser. VIII (1956), pp. 280–95, for indications of involuntary underemployment in the pre-industrial revolution economy.

the interpretation appears to be marred by both a major omission and an element of self-contradiction in the argument. The element of self-contradiction arises because employers do not complain of a shortage of labour when there is also a deficiency in demand. Charges of laziness and recalcitrance on the part of workers appear when the level of activity is high, not when it is low. This paradox could be resolved if the situation induced by the redistribution of income was one in which the demand for manufactures had fallen but the supply of labour to produce them had fallen still further. However, this is implausible. Such a situation would be completely unlike the one that obviously prevailed in agriculture and produced similar charges of idleness. Within agriculture, activity certainly increased. The price fall itself depended upon larger crops actually being harvested. Even if the extra output came from the bounty of nature, it had to be gathered by the industry of man. For this reason the phrase 'agricultural depression' is misleading. The situation can be more accurately described as a cost-price squeeze exerted upon the farmer. On the one side he was confronted by falling prices and on the other by sticky rents and rising wage rates. Certainly the position of the agricultural labourer was not depressed. Not only did he gain from falling prices but also his wage rates seem to have risen and it is possible that given a high demand for labour earnings may have risen faster than rates. There is little wonder that he was blackguarded by his employer. In order to assert that the situation of labour within manufacturing was different from that in agriculture it is necessary to postulate either an asymmetry in the behaviour of agricultural and domestic workers or some reallocation of labour away from manufacturing and towards agriculture. Perhaps agricultural workers were easier to coerce or bribe than domestic workers but any marked contrast seems unlikely in view of contemporary complaints that domestic workers were increasing their consumption of groceries and other luxuries. Moreover, domestic workers showed a willingness to migrate in response to economic incentives and this seems inconsistent with a character of unambitious sloth.[1] The paradox of simultaneously alleging low demand and labour scarcity cannot be convincingly resolved in this way.

[1] For a view of the eighteenth century labourer that has influenced the argument of this section at several points see A. H. John, 'Agricultural Productivity and Economic Growth in England, 1700–1760', *Journ. Econ. Hist.* XXV (1965), pp. 19–34.

However, if we completely reverse Deane and Cole's interpretation of the effects of falling agricultural prices and, instead, see the price fall as stimulating rather than depressing the economy, the evidence of labour scarcity can be interpreted without paradox. On this reading the complaints about the idleness of workers arose because the demand for manufactured goods had increased, thus exerting pressure in the labour market: the supply of labour expanded but its expansion was inadequate to accommodate the wishes of employers. Such an interpretation has the advantage that it makes thoroughly consistent the contemporary charges that workers were both idle and self-indulgent in luxuries at times of glut. It also makes the situation in manufacturing parallel to that in agriculture where charges of idleness were made in times of high not low activity. However, in order to sustain this interpretation it is necessary to overcome Deane and Cole's central objection that falling agricultural prices were more likely to depress than stimulate manufacturing because they caused a transfer of income from a high spending to a low spending group. A weakness of this diagnosis is that it is marred by a major omission: the impact effect of a fall in agricultural prices—resulting from an increase in agricultural output—would not be simply to redistribute income but also to increase real income for the community as a whole. Accordingly, in order to reduce demand for manufactures the redistribution effect—even if it were depressing—would have to outweigh the stimulating influence of a rise in real income. Moreover, it is doubtful whether the redistribution even in itself induced a fall in demand. Deane and Cole seem to use the concept 'marginal propensity to consume' in a special sense. They appear to imply that the labourer had a lower marginal propensity to consume than the farmer and landlord because he was willing to forgo income in favour of leisure. This is, of course, unlike the normal use of the concept in which marginal propensity is related to spending out of income received. In their sense of the term, the view that the labourer had a lower marginal propensity to consume has already been challenged in our earlier discussion. There seems little reason to believe that labourers merely passively received the benefit of the price fall translating some of it into leisure. Instead it seems more plausible that they were coerced or bribed into working harder for yet additional income. As we have seen, this must have occurred in

agriculture for the crops to be gathered and it is the only consistent way of reading contemporary criticism about domestic
workers. The implication is clear. Even in itself the redistribution
effect was not depressing. Accordingly, the consequence of a good
harvest was probably to raise demand since it involved a neutral
distribution effect combined with an upward real income effect.[1]
As in the early nineteenth century, it seems likely that in themselves good harvests stimulated the economy.[2] But beyond this
the view that has been argued for is that—for whatever reason—
activity was actually increased. This appears to be the most
plausible explanation of the contemporary charges that the work
force was at once both lazy and self-indulgent. Such a view of
high activity conflicts not only with Deane and Cole's analysis
of the effects of low agricultural prices but also with their general
picture of the period before 1745 as one of stagnation.

At first sight this may seem an unacceptable conclusion because
it is at variance not merely with Deane and Cole's analysis but
also with their interpretation of a substantial body of data.
However, as we shall see, their weighting and interpretation of the
evidence is itself open to question. Indeed, the evidence seems to
conflict with, rather than support, the hypothesis of a turning-
point in the 1740s once the *prima facie* case for a turning-point
at this time is removed. In evaluating Deane and Cole's presenta-
tion of the evidence it is important to notice that they adopt on
several occasions a procedure that could only be justified if the
case for a turning-point had already been made out. They frequently measure rates of growth to and from the presumed
turning-point. Consequently, they are able to document marked
discontinuities in percentage rates of growth. However, such
discontinuities are bound to appear in any series exhibiting
cyclical fluctuations where a period starting at a normal or high
year and ending with a low year is compared with one starting at
a low year and ending with a normal or high year. For example a

---

[1] Other factors could, of course, be introduced into the argument but it is not clear how,
on balance, they would affect its conclusion. For example, on the one hand, farmers and
landlords may have contracted their borrowings because of falling real incomes (although
it is not certain that the real income of landlords fell). Against this, the increased exports
of agricultural products would have helped to ease monetary conditions within the
economy.

[2] For an analysis of the effects of harvest variation in the early nineteenth century, see
R. C. O. Matthews, *A Study in Trade-cycle History: Economic Fluctuations in Great Britain
1833–1842* (Cambridge, 1954).

comparison is made between, on the one hand, the period 1700–1745 and, on the other, the periods 1745–1771 and 1745–1760. Indeed, the choice of 1700 to compare with the trough year of 1745 is explicitly made because the years on either side were depressed![1]

The most comprehensive quantitative information relating to English industry in the eighteenth century is the data for that part of its input and output which entered into foreign trade. Understandably, Deane and Cole give this evidence a substantial weight in their assessment of the economy.[2] However, the major series upon which they rely is one giving the addition of domestic exports and retained imports. This seems an unsatisfactory choice for two reasons. First, because the export series is much more accurate than the import series since—as Deane and Cole acknowledge—it was much less influenced by smuggling.[3] Moreover—again as they point out—the smuggling was not uniform in its incidence through time but depressed the official values of trade particularly at the time of the major turning-points in the series.[4] Second, the import figures only very partially reflect the changing production of English industry either directly or indirectly. They do not properly reflect it directly because there is a heavy weight of final consumer goods in the import bill. They do not do so indirectly because the volume of imports changes with both the terms of trade and capital movements and not merely with the growing volume of English exports. The countervailing weakness of the export series—that it may not have grown in step with domestic production—is important but it seems a good deal less significant than the deficiencies of the import series. Moreover, it is a deficiency that is not necessarily offset by an import series even of raw materials since part of this would reflect imports that were substitutes for domestic production and not complements to it. Accordingly, it seems better to use the series for domestic exports as an indication of the growth of domestic industry rather than add to it the series for retained imports. However, a still better series is probably obtained by making some allowance for re-exports since these reflect the expansion of important activities such as shipping and the associated activities such as shipbuilding.

[1] Deane and Cole, op. cit. p. 49.
[2] Ibid., pp. 41–50.
[3] Ibid., pp. 44–5.
[4] Ibid., p. 45.

In order to make this allowance a series of domestic exports plus fifteen per cent of re-exports has been prepared. This export series becomes a poor indicator of domestic progress towards the end of the eighteenth century and during the nineteenth. For the last part of the eighteenth century and the first half of the nineteenth, Britain's pioneer position, particularly in cotton, enabled her exports to rise much more rapidly than any plausible values that could be assigned to overall production.[1] Moreover, there is an independent reason why exports in this period exaggerate domestic growth. This is because exports become increasingly dominated by an item—manufactured cottons—that had a below average 'domestic value added' component.[2] However, for most of the eighteenth century the combined export series probably represents the best indicator of the advance of domestic industry.

Using the series for domestic exports plus fifteen per cent re-exports and comparing like years, a picture emerges of the first seventy-five years of the century that is strikingly different from the one presented by Deane and Cole. From 1700[3] to 1737—from the good years at the beginning of the century to the best year before the weakening of the 1740s—exports grew by 1·4 per cent per annum. From 1737 to 1771—a comparably high year before the American Revolution—growth was also at 1·4 per cent per annum. Comparing trough years the case against a turning-point is even stronger. From 1703 to 1744 the yearly growth rate was 1·3 per cent whereas between 1744 and 1780 it was only 0·5 per cent. The same pattern emerges from the movement of domestic exports without any allowance for re-exports.[4] Whether the comparison is made between peak years or between trough years the growth in the first period before 1745 is faster than in the middle period, i.e. before the boom of 1771 or the trough of 1780. Not until the 1780s does any marked increase occur in the growth of exports. However, whether the rapid expansion at this time marks a turning-point for the economy as a whole is—for the reasons given above—open to considerable doubt. But for the

[1] Ibid., p. 311.
[2] It is possible to compensate roughly for this defect by subtracting approximately ten per cent from cotton exports. When this is done the effect on the growth of exports in the early nineteenth century is quite substantial but the acceleration in export growth—mainly due to cotton—remains during the late eighteenth and early nineteenth centuries.
[3] In each case the date given is the mid-point of a three-year average.
[4] The annual percentage growth rate of domestic exports is: 1700–1737, *1·4*; 1737–1771, *0·9*; 1703–1744, *0·7*; 1744–1780, *0·6*.

first three-quarters of the century there is a clear indication from the foreign trade figures that throughout the whole period growth was taking place over a wide front and at more than a negligible rate.

It must be acknowledged that the first half of the century makes a poorer showing on the evidence of the excise series and other indicators of domestic output. However, the available information on this subject may well be misleading. Much of it was inaccurately collected because of evasion, inefficiency or bias. Some of it relates solely to old-established parts of the country and therefore excludes what may have been the faster growing centres. Some estimates are based on imports which may themselves be inaccurately recorded and even if accurate may not reflect the value of domestic output. An example of the probable defects of available estimates of output is provided by the germinal iron industry. The estimates of output have been criticised and it has been cogently argued that the industry was by no means stagnating in the first half of the century.[1] As a whole the output series take little account of precisely those industries where —according to the trade figures—the most rapid developments were taking place. An important aspect of the export figures is not merely their aggregate change but also the increase in their diversity and sophistication in the first half of the century. From being virtually dependent upon one manufactured export in 1700 England had established by mid-century an export trade based on new manufactured products, sold in new—largely colonial— markets, in exchange for non-manufactured products. On the basis of a detailed examination of trade figures during the eighteenth century it was recently concluded that:

'The process of industrialization in England from the second quarter of the eighteenth century was to an important extent a response to colonial demands for nails, axes, firearms, buckets, coaches, clocks, saddles, handkerchiefs, buttons, cordage and a thousand other things . . .'[2]

The export of these goods was not in negligible amounts.[3] Of the

[1] M. W. Flinn, 'Revisions in Economic History, XVII, The Growth of the English Iron Industry, 1660–1760', *Econ. Hist. Rev.* 2nd ser. XI (1958), pp. 144–53.

[2] See R. Davis, 'English Foreign Trade 1700–1744', *Econ. Hist. Rev.* 2nd ser. XV (1962), pp. 285–303.

[3] The revised estimates of manufactured exports presented by Davis, ibid. are of considerable importance in evaluating the significance of foreign trade as a factor both reflecting and influencing the advance of the economy.

140 per cent increase in the export of manufactured goods
between 1699–1701 and 1772–4, over three-quarters was contributed by non-woollen manufactures.[1] Perhaps the diversity of the
advance has told against its recognition by those who associate
rapid growth with a dominant leading sector but it is difficult to
see what distinguishes it from growth in the late eighteenth
century either intrinsically or as an agent promoting further
growth.

In the case of the still predominant agricultural sector there are
only indirect and unsatisfactory indicators of output. However,
the once held notion of near stagnation until the second half of the
eighteenth century—derived in large part from the numbers of
parliamentary enclosures—has been dispelled by a considerable
volume of detailed research.[2] This has revealed extensive and
considerable changes in agriculture during the seventeenth and
early eighteenth century. Indeed the fall in agricultural prices
during the first half of the eighteenth century can be plausibly
attributed to the spread of new techniques. That this price fall
created distress among farmers—even among all farmers—is no
reason for believing that innovation was not responsible for it.
In a competitive industry it may well continue to be profitable for
each individual producer to introduce a new technique even
though the effect of its wide adoption is to worsen the position
of every producer. This can easily occur in a situation such as the
one that prevailed in English agriculture where (a) there are fixed
charges to be met beyond those associated with the new technique
and (b) demand for the product of the industry is inelastic. In
these circumstances a fall in price will accompany innovation and
this may squeeze profits for the group as a whole even though
each individual producer would be still worse off if he refused to
adopt the new technique. As Deane and Cole suggest there is
little doubt that the percentage increase in the volume of agricultural output was substantially greater in the second half of the
century than in the first. For agriculture the volume of output was
undoubtedly geared to a major extent to the size of population.
Given the limited opportunities to export, the limited possibility
of variation in food intake per head and the limited industrial

---

[1] Ibid., p. 290.
[2] See especially E. L. Jones, 'Agriculture and Economic Growth in England, 1700–1750:
Agricultural Change', *Journ. Econ. Hist.* XXV (1965), pp. 1–18.

demand for English agricultural products, this must have been so. However, this is not sufficient reason to draw a sharp contrast between the dynamism of the industry in the first and second part of the century. It is a moot point whether it shows greater dynamism to undertake a technological revolution in the face of an inelastic demand situation or to accommodate to a substantial widening of the market without a marked change in techniques and this seems to be the true contrast between the two periods:

'Between the middle of the seventeenth century and the middle of the eighteenth century, English agriculture underwent a transformation in its techniques out of all proportion to the rather limited widening of its market . . . Except in the sphere of stockbreeding, the remainder of the century really had little to offer in the way of techniques which were new in principle.'[1]

Moreover, in evaluating the role of agriculture in the economy during this period the change in productivity seems a more important test than the change in output. Except for a major exporter of agricultural products one would normally judge the contribution of agriculture to overall economic growth by its success in releasing labour to the rest of the economy in a situation where population is stationary. Even though there are no direct estimates of productivity available it seems inescapable that if the fact of a technological revolution has any meaning there must either have been an increase in productivity and/or a much larger increase in output than Deane and Cole allow. As we shall see the index of output they have constructed almost certainly understates the increase in output but probably not sufficiently to remove the presumption of productivity advance. It seems likely that by adopting the criterion of output change Deane and Cole have undervalued the importance of agricultural change in the first half of the century but it also seems likely that in detail their account understates progress in the sector and its importance for the rest of the economy.[2] They stress parliamentary enclosure without setting it against a background of enclosure by agreement. The index of output they construct is based on an sssumption of unchanged consumption per capita in both quantity and quality. No account is taken of the important role of horses in the

[1] Ibid., p. 1.
[2] Some additional concessions to gradualness appear in Phyllis Deane, op. cit. but a marked contrast is still drawn between the progress in the first and second half of the century.

economy within and outside agriculture and therefore—in turn—
of the importance of an increase in their fodder supply.[1] Changes
in the seasons are emphasized rather than technical improvements.
Although qualifications are introduced at various points, the
marked technical change, important geographical reorganization,
substantial enclosure and considerable investment in the first half
of the century—all of which have been noted in recent studies—
receive little if any mention. When these aspects are taken into
account it seems very likely that in agriculture like manufacturing
there was cumulative, sustained significant advance before 1750.
Neither individually nor collectively, neither in intention nor
effect, do the actors in the economic drama seem a different
species in the first part of the eighteenth century from those in the
second; nor do the differences in degree seem greater than those
between say 1800 and 1850, 1850 and 1900, or 1900 and 1950.

Both the attempt to document a fundamental turning-point
in the 1740s[2] and the attempt to construct a model of the economy
that would make such a turning-point plausible are unconvincing.
But beyond this Deane and Cole's version of the turning-point
hypothesis seems to have a radical weakness since—when their
model and its implications are seen in perspective—it is not clear
in what sense, if any, they have provided even a *possible* explanation of a fundamental point of inflexion in the growth path. In
order to substantiate this let us assume that their turning-point
mechanism is completely accepted. That development in England
was held back during the 1730s and 1740s by a shortage of demand
and—as the other side of the same coin—by a shortage of labour;
and, that these restraints were then broken by the combination
of an increase in population and a run of bad harvests so that
England was launched into self-sustained growth through the
increased toil of labourers and the increased expenditure of landlords and farmers. In some respects such an analysis represents an
inversion of the Malthusian trap forces that are commonly
pictured as restraining the advance of underdeveloped economies
and whose reversal is held to be likely to generate a sudden leap
forward in growth. Stagnation prevails in the Malthusian situation

---

[1] A. H. John, op. cit. p. 28.
[2] The discussion has concentrated throughout on the turning-point of the 1740s. Deane
and Cole refer occasionally to the possibility of other turning-points. However, their
whole treatment and emphasis leaves no doubt that for them this is the period in which
the *fundamental* change occurred in the economy.

because at low standards of living any rise in income is over-matched by a rise in population thus restoring per capita income to its equilibrium level. By contrast in the leisure preference situation a rise in population is necessary to free the economy from an inelastic labour supply through a redistribution of income away from the labourers to more sophisticated groups. Although it would be misleading to apply a simple version of the Malthusian model to the English economy it is certain that society had been racked on a number of occasions by Malthusian crises. Pressure on food supplies had occurred often enough before the 1750s. The novel feature of the situation in the eighteenth century was the change in the response of the economy to this pressure and not the pressure itself. Moreover, the crucial changes that governed this response may well have considerably antedated the application of the pressure. Accordingly Deane and Cole's emphasis is inappropriate for two reasons. First, it directs attention to recurrent forces to explain a fundamental change and thus distracts from what was unique in the situation. Second, it directs attention to the point of time when response occurred and thus distracts from the events by which the response was conditioned. It may be useful to enlarge upon the interpretation of their model which is implied in this criticism. If we accept the notion of a fundamental turning-point in English development occurring around the mid-eighteenth century it becomes necessary to explain what forces had previously inhibited growth. Malthusian forces are a possible candidate for this role but they are unlikely to have continuously impeded previous growth because of the wide and long swings that occurred in the food/population balance during previous centuries. The upward swings would have carried the economy clear of the trap unless some other constraint was involved. However, by supplementing Malthusian forces by a desired income ceiling on the output of goods and services a model can be built up which produces stagnation without any necessity to postulate a rapid adjustment of the food/population balance. The ceiling of desired income is imposed by leisure preference and fluctuations around it take place because of variations in population and food supply. Movements above the ceiling are only in potential income since actual income is exchanged for leisure. Movements below the ceiling are in actual income and produce varying degrees of discomfort which at their worst constitute

Malthusian crises. In terms of this model the change between the 1730s and 1750s is merely one more—rather minor—turn in a continuous alternation around the desired income ceiling. Accordingly, even if Deane and Cole's analysis of the 1740s were to be accepted it seems much more plausible to see it as an explanation of one more of a long series of cycles and in no sense— in itself—representing an explanation of fundamental change in the structure or performance of the economy.

IV

It has been argued in this paper that a fundamental turning-point is unlikely to be a feature of evolutionary growth and does not occur in the English case. If these arguments are accepted they involve discarding the turning-point concept as a tool of historical analysis. Beyond this, their acceptance makes it necessary to re-consider the relationship between the study of past and present development that seems to be implied in recent studies.

One of the attractions of the turning-point hypothesis is that it appears to suggest an approach to the unification of the study of historical and contemporary development by treating the English industrial revolution as closely comparable with the transition to self-sustained growth in contemporary under-developed countries. However, on examination, it is not clear how much is being implied by this comparison. One of the few explicit statements of the implications of the analogy occurs in a recent essay by Deane and Cole:

'Nor is the controversy about the concept of a "take-off" merely a dispute about words and definitions. For countries which have not yet begun to enjoy the benefits of rapid economic growth the question of whether it is possible to define a "take-off" stage in the growth process, to identify a period and concatenation of events which, once successfully completed, ensure a perpetual tendency for real incomes per head to increase, is obviously a question of peculiar interest.'[1]

Taken literally this seems a curious view. As far as the example of already developed countries is concerned it would seem that the only assurance that underdeveloped countries can secure is the

[1] Phyllis Deane and W. A. Cole, 'The Growth of National Income', p. 10, in *The Cambridge Economic History*, Vol. IV, Part 1, ed. H. J. Habakkuk and M. Postan (Cambridge, 1965).

readily obtainable one that substantial growth rates can be achieved in these—different—settings; whether or not the historian can make a judgement about the point of time at which growth becomes self-sustaining in these already developed economies appears to have no practical significance. Of course, Deane and Cole's remarks may imply that it is helpful to identify turning points if they are marked by a *similar* concatenation of events in each case and this does, indeed, go to the root of the matter. Discontinuities in growth could arise for a large number of reasons. Yet, as we have seen, apart from Rostow's pioneering thesis, no attempt has been made to demonstrate that turning-points occur for similar reasons in different economies. Accordingly, not much would seem to follow immediately by way of either illumination or prescription even if a number of turning-points were identified.

Making policy prescriptions on the basis of their success in another economy is obviously dangerous unless it can be shown that the two economies are alike in the relevant respects. Economists have been rightly castigated for prescribing for under-developed countries on the basis of models designed for diagnosing the ills of advanced economies.[1] At first sight it might seem that these objections do not apply where prescriptions for contemporary developing countries are based upon the experience of already developed economies at the time they underwent an industrial revolution. Certainly such prescriptions are common. Thus historical experience, and particularly English experience in the eighteenth century, has been used as one of the major supports for adopting a strategy of unbalanced growth in developing countries.[2] Again, the telling historical example is often used to confirm the importance of heavy industry or light industry, tariffs or expansion through trade, agriculture or manufacturing, in the development process. However, the use of these 'historical lessons' to support policy prescriptions is extremely misleading. First, underdeveloped areas are themselves diverse. Certain characteristics of an economy—such as the proportion of the

[1] D. Seers, 'The Limitations of the Special Case', *Bulletin of the Oxford University Institute of Economics and Statistics* (1963), pp. 77–98.

[2] See P. Streeten, *Economic Integration* (Leyden, 1961), pp. 118–23; T. Scitovsky, 'Growth—Balanced or Unbalanced?', in *The Allocation of Economic Resources*, ed. M. Abramovitz et al. (Stanford, 1959), pp. 207–17; and R. B. Sutcliffe, 'Balanced and Unbalanced Growth', *Quart. Journ. of Econ.* (1964), pp. 621–40, who, however, advances some important criticisms of the historical analogy.

workforce engaged in agriculture—are closely correlated with the level of average income and therefore tend to distinguish important aspects of the structure of underdeveloped areas, as a group, from those of developed areas. But the differences in *per capita* incomes between various underdeveloped countries is itself considerable. For example, in percentage terms the difference in average income between Pakistan and Malaya is probably greater than between Malaya and the United Kingdom. Moreover, there are a host of characteristics that may be relevant to policy prescriptions such as dependence upon foreign trade—which are not closely correlated with average income. Second, and more fundamental, the *ex post* pattern of development achieved under evolutionary growth is an inappropriate guide to policy measures. The pattern of development emerges as a result of decisions to expand in particular sectors taken in the light of an assessment of the responsiveness of factor supplies, intermediate goods and demand to this expansion. However, prescriptions to expand through leading sectors—or in some particular sector such as heavy industry—because that pattern has occurred elsewhere, seem based on the assumption that once these sectors are initiated in an underdeveloped economy their initiation will itself guarantee adequate response. A manifestation of growth in an historical situation is treated as an agent of growth in a contemporary situation.

Clearly, development studies and economic history can be mutually illuminating. Indeed, in many respects they can be regarded as the same discipline. However, this does not mean that economists should expect to discover historical situations that so closely parallel contemporary situations that they suggest straightforward lessons for growth. Indeed, it is not cynical to take the opposite view that the chief value of historical studies should be to immunize economists against a too ready acceptance of the lessons of history by making them conscious of the peculiarity of each case: to condition them to examine the structure of each economy before predicting a particular pattern of growth or predicting a particular response to policy measures. This seems to apply particularly to the use of the English industrial revolution as the source of historical lessons. As the first example of transition to self-sustained growth it is the most studied and the most familiar. Yet precisely because it is the first—and therefore the most completely evolutionary case—it is probably the least helpful of any as an example of how to grow.

It has been well said that: 'In humane studies there are times when a new error is more life-giving than an old truth, a fertile error than sterile accuracy.'[1] Unfortunately, the turning-point hypothesis—although undoubtedly stimulating—tends to confirm the major traditional and contemporary misconceptions that beset students of the industrial revolution: that the revolution represented a sudden sharp discontinuity in growth and that historical and contemporary development are not merely mutually illuminating but provide near duplicates of one another. In this sense —as we have argued—it tends to cloud the major contributions of recent economic and statistical studies.

[1] H. R. Trevor-Roper, *History: Professional and Lay* (Oxford, 1957), p. 22.

2

R. M. HARTWELL

Business Management in England during the Period of Early Industrialization: Inducements and Obstacles

I

A major interest of economists since 1945 has been to measure, or at least to rank, the relative contributions to economic growth of increasing inputs of the productive factors on the one hand, and of increasing efficiency on the other. When M. Abramovitz in a famous article[1] showed that most of the increases in net product per capita in the United States since 1870 was the result of inputs *other than* inputs of physical capital stock and the services of labour, he started 'the great *Residual* hunt', the search for those factors which raise productivity rather than those which expand resource inputs. And although his and the many other studies of growth which now exist have used unreliable statistical data processed under assumptions of heroic simplicity, their conclusions are the same: for the period of modern statistics, i.e. since the third quarter of the nineteenth century, increases in per capita product have been the result of increasing the efficiency rather than the volume of resources.[2] Unfortunately the economists have failed to identify conclusively the constituent elements of the *Residual*, although some have argued persuasively for technical progress and investment in human capital.[3] Historians have not had the disadvantage, in seeking the sources of increasing output over the ages, of the intellectual strait-jacket of a preposterously simple growth model, and so have long recognised the growth

---

[1] 'Resource and Output Trends in the United States since 1870', *American Economic Review* (1956).

[2] See, particularly, the work of S. Kuznets, J. W. Kendrick, S. Fabricant, E. Denison, etc.

[3] R. W. Solow, 'Technical Progress, Capital Formation and Economic Growth', and T. W. Schultz, 'Investment in Human Capital', *American Economic Review* (1961 and 1962).

roles of both resource inputs and improved productivity. As K. F. Helleiner pointed out in 1946: 'It would be difficult to decide whether man in the course of history has achieved more through making additions to his land, or through improved utilization of his available soil.'[1] However, over much of history, when economic organization and technology were relatively static, and when the dominant economic activity was agriculture, output was expanded mainly by increases of population and by the colonization of new land; by having more people, with more of the same simple tools, till more land. There were occasionally significant improvements in the efficiency of production, such as that marked by the invention of agriculture, but the industrial revolution was a major turning-point in the history of increasing output after which increasing efficiency became generally more important than increasing resource inputs. Before this, as the slow growth of output attests, it was usually inputs which were more important. And on the industrial revolution the historians, although as a collectivity they have had an eclectic explanation of the rise of English output, have emphasized, realistically, the increasing efficiency of the economy: the attention given to increasing inputs (more land cultivated, more minerals mined, more labour employed, more capital equipment) has been far less than analysis of the productivity gains of transferring production from the home or the workshop to the factory (and thus, generally, of substituting power-driven improved metal machinery for hand-worked primitive wooden machinery), and of centralizing ownership and management in the person of the capitalist-entrepreneur. These changes have been summed up, by the historians, in the phrase 'the factory system'.

'The factory system', wrote P. Mantoux, 'concentrates and multiplies the means of production so that the output is both accelerated and increased.' 'The manufacturer, being at the same time a capitalist, a works manager and a merchant, sets a new pattern of the complete business man.'[2] 'The manufacturer' was a new type of business organizer; 'the factory' was a new type of business organization. This was recognized by contemporaries, and subsequently by historians, who for long have lavished praise

[1] *Readings in European Economic History* (Toronto, 1946), p. 29.
[2] P. Mantoux, *The Industrial Revolution in the Eighteenth Century* (London, 1928, English Edition), p. 386.

on the great industrial revolution entrepreneurs, especially the great technical innovators. The emphasis has been, however, on technology; on the role of the new manufacturers as organization-innovators there has been reticence or silence; attention has focused on the machine, rather than on the factory which housed it. Technical change has been described in great detail; organizational change has been discussed, and then only briefly, in terms, usually, of the advantages of the economies of scale. And the gains of scale have been seen, not so much as the explicit gains of managerial competence, but rather as the wind-fall gains of machine technology. For example, it is obviously important to think of the invention of the factory as a crucial step in the industrialization of England. However, although there has been some discussion of early factories, the pioneering importance of John and Thomas Lombe who in 1719 built the first modern textile factory of the industrial revolution is barely recognized, although there is one short article on them.[1]

Economists now recognize the central role in economic change of the entrepreneur, and also explain productivity differences between factories, industries and economies partly, at least, in terms of managerial-organizational differences.[2] Historians have not been so explicit. Organization is certainly more difficult to describe than machinery, and the evidence which historians have to demonstrate its changing character is elusive and difficult to interpret. For these reasons, management has been discussed rarely (with one notable exception) as a subject in its own right; rather it has appeared at a highly generalized level, or in terms of particular managerial problems. At the elevated level of the stage-builders, for example, 'the factory system' has been seen as one of an orderly sequence of evolutionary stages of organization; and, to those who divide history into periods, each characterized by a distinctive ethos or spirit, the factory emerged in the period of 'economic rationality' and 'individualism'. More typical, however, has been the discussion of *problems of management and organization*: in particular, the two problems of capital accumula-

---

[1] 'Sir Thomas Lombe (1685–1739) and the British Silk Industry', in W. H. Chaloner, *People and Industries* (London, 1963), pp. 8–20. Also see Mantoux, op. cit., p. 198.
[2] As C. P. Kindleberger (*Economic Development*, 2nd ed., New York, 1965, p. 118) notes: 'in modern Egyptian factories, technologically the equal to those in the United States, labour productivity is one-sixth to one-fourth that of the United States, a difference attributed to differences in the quantity and quality of organization'.

tion and industrial relations have received considerable attention from the historians of the industrial revolution. Capital accumulation has been linked with management through the importance of abstinence and the ploughing-back of profits, both managerial qualities for success in this period. The problems of industrial relations have been seen mainly as problems of labour recruitment and training, and have been considered more as the province of the history of labour, as part of 'the making of the English working class',[1] than as part of the history of management. Only S. Pollard has placed both problems in the explicit context of a long and detailed account of 'the genesis of modern management'. But Pollard's conclusion is surprising: 'Perhaps the most important conclusion to emerge is that "management" . . . , though not a barrier to progress, yet could not be shown to have been an initiator of change either. The pragmatic discovery of new methods was no doubt adequate, but management appears everywhere to have adapted itself merely to the needs of technology, discipline or financial control. Among the many competing explanations there can surely nowhere be a managerial theory of industrial revolutions.'[2] Such a conclusion contrasts not only with what economists have discovered about modern growth, but also with Pollard's own detailed account of management problems during the industrial revolution and how they were solved.

It is difficult, certainly, to separate technical progress from capital accumulation during the industrial revolution, and technical change almost invariably involved changed organization; to this extent the decision to invest automatically involved decisions also about organization. But that these latter decisions were important should be obvious: the character and success of those who survived the very high failure rate among the early industrialists can be explained, not so much in terms of differences in the quality of labour or of machines, but more in terms of differences in the quality of management.[3] It is important to

[1] The title of an important book by Mr E. P. Thompson.

[2] S. Pollard, *The Genesis of Modern Management. A Study of the Industrial Revolution in England* (London, 1965), p. 271.

[3] H. Burgess (*Parliamentary Papers*, 1836 (465) viii, part 2, p. 365) reckoned about industry generally that between 1819 and 1836, 9 out of 10 of the great manufacturing works had changed hands. R. Baker, the factory inspector (ibid., 1847 (779) xv, letter of 7 November 1846) estimated that of 318 firms in his district in 1836, only 127 were still in operation in 1846.

remember, also, that during the English industrial revolution, more than in any subsequent industrialization, the one man often combined two or more of the roles of capitalist, inventor, innovator and manager, so that high success demanded wide ability. Richard Arkwright is an outstanding example of technical and managerial innovator. As R. S. Fitton and A. P. Wadsworth affirm, 'The decision to go to Cromford and apply water power to machinery still far from perfect was one of the turning-points in the history of the factory system.'[1] At Cromford, Arkwright built a factory for his own newly-invented machinery, and created a new type of community (the cotton factory village), and managed both with such success that he became wealthy and famous, and was widely imitated. Where one great innovator led, others followed, and it was the host of imitators, with roughly the same spectrum of advantages and disadvantages, who constituted the on-going impetus to the industrial revolution. Whatever the qualities of the initiators of change, the success of imitators was more dependent on good management than on the machines and labourers they so assiduously tended with such varying results.

II

The context of this inquiry into the development of business management in the period of early industrialization is in terms of 'inducements and obstacles'; i.e. in the now common context of discussion about contemporary under-development in terms of 'obstacles to industrialization'.[2] Having established the importance of management and organizational change as a factor in England's industrial revolution, it is necessary to ask what determined the supply of entrepreneur-managers, and whether or not entrepreneurs were seriously limited in their activities by social and economic restraints? Was there a shortage of entrepreneurs? What were the inducements to enterprise? Were entrepreneurs faced with formidable obstacles? Is it possible to draw a balance sheet of inducements and obstacles? On the supply of entre-

---

[1] R. S. Fitton and A. P. Wadsworth, *The Strutts and the Arkwrights* (Manchester, 1958), p. 98. See, also, J. P. Addis, *The Crawshay Dynasty* (Cardiff, 1957), for an interesting account of the evolution of an innovating manufacturing family, with origins in merchanting.

[2] For example, *Processes and Problems of Industrialization in Under-Developed Countries* (United Nations, New York, 1955).

preneurs it is doubtful that any argument, or proof, can be produced to demonstrate shortage. 'They came', as Charles Wilson has argued, 'from every social source and every area.'[1] They flourished, and failed, in every variety of enterprise. 'Like a newly discovered gold mine', Mantoux wrote, 'the factory system attracted men from all over the country.'[2] But what of the environment in which they strove and competed? In a very general way historians have argued that there is a functional relationship between entrepreneurship and the social structure and value-system of the society in which they live and work. The argument is that some societies are more encouraging to enterprise than others. As A. Gerschenkron has written: 'The theoretical formula is persuasively simple: social approval of entrepreneurial activity significantly affects its volume and quality.'[3] Certainly the socio-political environment of eighteenth century England was a favourable one for entrepreneurial endeavour. Generally, as Witt Bowden has pointed out, entrepreneurs were held 'in high esteem'; and the great industrialists were men of 'great wealth and opulence, and of great power and influence arising from that wealth and opulence', and men whose status and importance was recognized and rewarded.[4] The century and a half between 1700 and 1850, also, was a period of great social mobility, when humble men of talent could aspire to, and attain, riches and social prestige, and even a title. As E. W. Gilboy has written, 'The changing economic structure occurring with widespread development of factories enabled many of [the working classes] to assume positions of responsibility in the industrial world'.[5] There was, as Leslie Stephen argued, 'the absence of . . . sharp lines of demarcation between classes and of . . . exclusive aristocratic privileges'; the men who were 'the chief instruments' of the industrial revolution were 'self-made' and 'owed nothing to government or to the

[1] Charles Wilson, 'The Entrepreneur in the Industrial Revolution', *The Experience of Economic Growth*, ed. B. E. Supple (New York, 1963), p. 182.

[2] P. Mantoux, *The Industrial Revolution in the Eighteenth Century*, op. cit., p. 376. See, for a particular industry, an account of the varied social origins of the ironmasters of the eighteenth century by T. S. Ashton (*Iron and Steel in the Industrial Revolution*, Manchester, 1924, pp. 209 *et seq.*).

[3] A. Gerschenkron, *Economic Backwardness in Historical Perspective* (Harvard University Press, 1966), p. 59.

[4] Witt Bowden, *Industrial Society in England towards the End of the Eighteenth Century* (London, 1965, 2nd edition), pp. 22, 160–1.

[5] E. W. Gilboy, *Wages in Eighteenth Century England* (Harvard University Press, 1934), p. 243.

universities which passed for the organs of national culture'; they sought and gained political power and became 'the backbone of the Whig party when it began to demand a serious reform'. Stephen concluded that, 'There is probably no period in English history at which a greater number of poor men have risen to distinction'.[1]

What, however, of the economic environment? The ability of entrepreneurs to effect a successful transformation of the economy depended basically on an increasingly efficient market which enabled economic behaviour, whether by consumers or producers, to be rationally 'satisfied' or 'rewarded', and hence to be encouraged. Obviously fundamental to market development was the increasing and more general economic rationality of behaviour; i.e. a maximizing behaviour towards work and wealth by an increasing number of people. However, while rationality, particularly its association with the Reformation and Protestantism, has been exhaustively, if not conclusively, debated, the equally important physical development of the market (in terms of communications and institutions) has been relatively, and curiously, neglected. The theme of the protestant origins of rationality has had the good fortune to have commanded the attention of some of the most formidable minds in economic history; for example, Max Weber and R. H. Tawney. Even so, after much research, writing and debate, doubts remain both about the necessary relationship between capitalism and religion, and about the primacy of ideas in the process of social change.[2] A basic dilemma is posed by the facts that capitalism has risen and flourished with and without protestantism, and that protestantism has risen and flourished with and without capitalism. It is by no means certain that exogenously changed values spurred men to greater and more effective effort, or, rather that successful enterprise created both the favourable environment for change, and the rationalization in values which favoured such enterprise. C. B. Macpherson has argued that, 'The essence of rational behaviour is industrious appropriation',[3] and certainly in England by the end of the seventeenth century a 'theory of possessive

---

[1] Leslie Stephen, *The English Utilitarians* (London, 1900), Vol. I, *Jeremy Bentham*, pp. 21, 61, 63, 111–12.

[2] See K. Samuelsson, *Religion and Economic Action* (English translation, London, 1961), for a critical summary of literature on 'religion and the rise of capitalism'.

[3] C. B. Macpherson, *The Theory of Possessive Individualism* (Oxford, 1962), p. 232.

individualism' had received articulate rationalization by John Locke, preparing the way for the economic liberalism of Adam Smith. But analysis at this general level of explanation does not enable us to understand the actions of individual entrepreneurs. To them the market and its institutions were all important; to operate effectively they needed a market with factor mobility and prices which reflected supply and demand conditions (so that factors were responsive to price incentives and had the ability to move); a market with consumers who maximized their satisfaction by buying according to price and quality differences; a market, also, in which 'true profits' could be earned (i.e. profits which included a margin above costs, including managerial costs, which 'measured' enterprise).[1] Many developments in the eighteenth century were combining, mutually reinforcing each other, to produce such a market. In the first place, in the century before 1760 the movement of goods, persons and information was much improved; all three moved more easily and more quickly. Improved communications 'valorized the hinterland' (as C. R. Fay once put it), greatly facilitated the movement of raw materials and finished goods, reduced the cost and increased the speed; the greatly extended use of stage waggons on the roads, and the rapid development of water transport, especially canals after mid-century, enormously boosted the carrying trade; for the first time in history a commodity and its transport—coal—was measured in millions of tons.[2] Some measure of mobility can be seen in the growth of towns and of industrial concentrations, and particularly

---

[1] The concept of profit in the eighteenth century was complicated by the fact that capitalist and manager-entrepreneur were, so often, the one person. For this reason profit was seen mainly as a return to capital; the idea of a management theory of profit did not come until much later. In most industrial revolution enterprises for which accounts have survived, profits were the residual after costs had been met, and were divided, in the case of partners, according to capital contributions. Only when enterprises came to depend mainly on borrowed capital, did attitudes towards profit change. A. Marshall, in particular, gave detailed consideration to the concept of profit: in *The Economics of Industry* (London, 1886) he discussed the relative advantages of trading on borrowed capital and on owned capital, noting that 'men with borrowed capital seem likely to displace to a great extent those trading with their own'; in *The Principles of Economics* (London, 1890), he argued, 'profits are something more than interest in addition to Net Earnings of Management'; i.e. those earnings which are properly to be ascribed to the abilities of business men. It is the Marshallian definition of profit that I use above.

[2] See W. T. Jackman, *The Development of Transportation in England* (London, 1916), for a detailed account of transport changes and the extent of the carrying trade; e.g. pp. 304–7; 310–12; 340–6; appendices 5 (on rate of travelling), 6 (on cost of travelling), and 7 (on cost of carriage of goods by land).

in the migration towards the north and west.[1] Such differential growth, between town and country, between region and region, reflected both the ability of labour and goods to move, but also the sensitivity of labour to wage incentives. As E. W. Gilboy has clearly demonstrated, England in the eighteenth century had 'a working population incited by changing wages and standards of life'; especially in the north, the workers were 'ambitious and active', 'with a growing taste for articles not heretofore included in their budget'.[2] Such motives allowed the expanding industrial centres to draw labour continuously from the countryside.[3]

Changing tastes and an increasing demand for goods were catered for by a rapidly growing mercantile community engaged in both internal and external trade. R. B. Westerfield has detailed the increase in merchants and the growing complexity of their operations and institutions in the century before the industrial revolution, showing their rate of increase to have been three to six times as great as that of total population. The growth of the market in size and sophistication can be seen, also, in the growth of shops at the expense of fairs and the old-type town markets. 'The rise of permanent shops', wrote Westerfield, 'was concomitant and causal to the relative decline of the public market and the travelling merchant and chapman. Middlemen increased in number and became sedentary'.[4] A good example of an individual manufacturer's response to changing market conditions is that of the Darbys of Coalbrookdale: the Darbys began, c. 1710, by selling iron-ware in small quantities to customers whom they met in person at fairs and country markets, and by taking orders at the great fairs at Chester and Stourbridge; by mid-century, to cater for a new type of customer, agents were employed in Cornwall and Northumberland; later still, as the industrial revolution got under way, warehouses were established in London, Bristol and Liverpool, holding stocks of goods for direct sale, and travellers were employed to make direct contact with purchasers,

[1] See Mantoux, op. cit., pp. 358–63, 365–6. For example, the population of Warwickshire and Staffordshire doubled, and that of Lancashire trebled, in the course of the eighteenth century. Manchester probably had 10,000 inhabitants in 1730, 27,000 in 1770, 50,000 in 1790 and 95,000 in 1801.

[2] E. W. Gilboy, *Wages in Eighteenth Century England* (Harvard, 1934), pp. 241–3.

[3] See A. Redford, *Labour Migration in England, 1800–1850* (Manchester, 1926) for an account of the process of migration during the industrial revolution.

[4] R. B. Westerfield, 'Middlemen in English Business, 1660–1760', *Transactions of the Connecticut Academy of Arts and Sciences*, vol. XIX, 1915, pp. 412, 414, 347.

especially large customers.[1] R. Davis, in particular, has documented the commercial organization of an expanding external trade, writing of the period 1635 to 1735, that, 'Nearly everywhere . . . change tended in the same direction. Nearly everywhere trade with England had greatly expanded . . . and the growth of this trade had led to, or has been accompanied by, the creation of a great network of English merchant houses or agencies abroad, closely linked with their homeland'.[2]

Financial change, to the extent that P. G. M. Dickson has entitled it a revolution, facilitated manufacturing and trade by more adequately providing currency and credit.[3] Improved and new financial institutions, particularly banks and insurance companies, laid the firmer foundations of a well integrated system of public and private finance. The development of the City of London as a capital and money market and as the nation's financial centre, with a complex network of complementary institutions, was important for the finance of industry, and for the finance of internal and external trade. Part of this financial growth was the establishment of a carefully organized and disciplined insurance sector which allowed the efficient offsetting of business risks, especially in international trade.[4] Better accounting, the result of better and more text-books on accounting,[5] and also of the general expansion of commercial education,[6] enabled more business men to get their costs and prices in a profitable (and competitive) relationship, with encouraging effects on enterprise and survival. Such financial and mercantile change ensured the emergence of a price-sophisticated consumer market, and a price-conscious manufacturing and mercantile community servicing that market. Increasing and keener competition everywhere sharpened wits, led to constant market skirmishing, and ensured the survival of the clever and well organized in an increasingly

---

[1] See A. Raistrick, *Dynasty of Iron Founders. The Darbys of Coalbrookdale* (London, 1953).

[2] R. Davis, *The Rise of the English Shipping Industry in the Seventeenth and Eighteenth Centuries* (London, 1962), p. 381.

[3] P. G. M. Dickson, *The Financial Revolution in England. A Study in the Development of Public Credit, 1688–1756* (London, 1967).

[4] For example, see P. G. M. Dickson, *The Sun Insurance Office, 1710–1960* (London, 1960) for an account of the development of one important office.

[5] For example, William Hamilton, *Book-keeping New Modelled: or, A Treatise on Merchants' Accounts* (Edinburgh, 1735). See books also by Roger North (1715), Alexander Brodie (1722), Richard Hayes (1739), Martin Clare (1751), William Gordon (1756), William Perry (1777), etc.

[6] N. A. Hans, *New Trends in Education in the Eighteenth Century* (London, 1951).

free domestic market. In the development of this free market, moreover, the activities of business men were reinforced by changes in law. Such changes took many forms: a decline occurred in the rights of the Crown in economic affairs (so that the Crown's once extensive powers to control, or to give to persons or corporations to control, internal trade were almost decadent when Blackstone wrote); the legislative fixing of prices and wages was abandoned as impracticable and undesirable; a range of statutes contributed to legal developments which favoured industry and commerce (by promoting domestic industry by fiscal expedients, by prohibiting the export of machines and artisans, by regulating colonial trade, etc.); there was a remarkable development of commercial law, especially under the influence of Lord Mansfield.[1] The general result was to incorporate into law the ideas and practices of the merchants and manufacturers, so that legal practice as regards contracts, negotiable instruments, bankruptcy, insurance, etc., was regularized and made certain. Thus wages and rents, the price of capital and the price of land, the price of raw materials and manufactured goods, all ceased to be determined either by custom or by market restrictions, and were determined, increasingly, by the relationship between supply and demand in a free market.

This picture, however, is too idyllic! Whatever their considerable advantages, the early entrepreneurs also faced formidable obstacles. If industrialization enhanced the chance of gain, it also increased the chance, and the cost, of failure. Increasing opportunities meant increasing risks: as new industries grew and localized, old industries declined and, with them, some areas;[2] firms were larger, with more capital equipment and longer inventories, so that more was at stake and failure was a more fearful prospect;[3] to crises induced by weather were added crises

[1] A legal history of the industrial revolution and its background has not been written, although volumes X, XI and XII of Sir William Holdsworth's *A History of English Law* (London, 1938) comes closest to such a history. See, for example: vol. X, on 'Local Government', p. 158 *et seq.* (for price and wage controls, turnpikes, improvement commissioners, etc.) and 'The Royal Prerogative', p. 400 *et seq.*; vol. XI on 'Colonies', p. 84 *et seq.*, on 'Statute Law' as regards manufactures and trade, p. 411 *et seq.*; vol. XII, on 'Equity' and the 'Common Law', especially as regards 'Commercial Law', p. 383 *et seq.*, and 'Maritime Law', p. 524 *et seq.*

[2] The textile industry in East Anglia all but perished; Durham became 'the home of lost industries'; Glasgow declined as a cotton centre; etc. See G. C. Allen, *British Industries and their Organization* (London, 1933), Ch. I.

[3] See, for example, T. S. Ashton, *Iron and Steel in the Industrial Revolution* (Manchester, 1924) on the increasing capital commitments of the iron masters; pp. 227–32.

produced regularly as a by-product of the new industry and trade;[1] the horizon of enterprise was greatly extended, and distant markets, often across fearful seas, made the production-sale cycle longer, the period of waiting for returns attenuated, expensive and nerve-racking;[2] there was a growing demand for goods not of basic necessity, whose demand was more elastic and uncertain, and was subject to changes in taste and fashion, so that any particular manufacturer's market could fluctuate wildly;[3] there was increasing technological uncertainty, as the rates of invention and technological improvement increased, and as the technological obsolescence increased;[4] there was, above all, increasing competition. All these factors can be summed up as increasing uncertainty and increasing risk; both became an essential component of business men's calculations. To such general obstacles should be added some specific problems which have been discussed in some detail by the historians. The shortage of coin is a good example: many manufacturers had difficulty in getting sufficient currency, especially small-unit coins for the payment of wages, for day-to-day commitments. Arkwright, for example, was forced to issue token coinage and to have Spanish dollars overstamped at Soho for use in his factory.[5] Shortage of coin was reinforced, often, by the difficulty of getting adequate short-term credit, a problem solved in the long run by the development of country banks, many of which had their origins in manufacturing.[6] There were, also, continuous technical problems, such as the servicing of new machines, the inadequacy of water power, and the imbalances caused by the differential technical progress of various processes.[7] The problem of labour discipline, of converting

[1] See, T. S. Ashton, *Economic Fluctuations in England, 1700–1800* (Oxford, 1959) for an account of the eighteenth century cycle.

[2] See R. Davis, *The Rise of the English Shipping Industry in the Seventeenth and Eighteenth Centuries* (London, 1962), for the risks of the shipping trade; pp. 375–6.

[3] Cotton textiles of varying fibre content and print design enabled, for the first time, a wide choice to the poorer consumers of textiles.

[4] See W. E. G. Salter, *Productivity and Technical Change* (Cambridge, 2nd ed., 1966), for discussion about technical change and 'the rate of improvement'.

[5] See Fitton and Wadsworth, op. cit., pp. 242–3, and Ashton, *Iron and Steel* . . . , op. cit., pp. 228–9, for examples of currency difficulties. Fitton and Wadsworth write (p. 244): 'New Lanark countermarked a 5s. Spanish dollar, a 2s. 6d. half-écu of France, a farthing on a William III Scottish bodle; Deanston used half-écus, Charles II bawbees, and George III halfpennies (countermarked 4s. 6d.); Ballindalloch and Rothesay had Spanish dollars, and so on. McConnel and Kennedy bought casks of coin from Boulton and Watt . . . and in 1812 their agents were scouring the country for silver'.

[6] For example, see Ashton (*Iron and Steel* . . . , op. cit.) on 'The Ironmasters'.

[7] Ibid., p. 99.

the agricultural labourer into industrial proletariat, has been sympathetically analysed by a number of historians who have tended to over-dramatize the problem but, nevertheless, who have demonstrated its formidable magnitude.[1] Many of these specific problems were new or substantially new; there was no 'heritage of improvement' to guide the entrepreneur in his strange new world; there was no advantage of 'the late start', no 'engine of growth' abroad to stimulate and prompt English growth, no important 'lessons of history' to be learnt. There was also, for many individual entrepreneurs, disapproval. As Mantoux has written: 'For its first eighty years the factory was on the defensive. It seemed to many an unnatural ogre'.[2] Opposition was both social and aesthetic. At first, however, the new factories were centres of interest and wonder. 'Coalbrookdale exercised a peculiar fascination over all who approached.'[3] 'The cotton mills [of Arkwright] of the Derwent Valley became one of the wonders of the Peak.'[4] Soon, however, wonder mixed with disapproval; the dales at Coalbrookdale lost 'all their beauties' as a 'variety of horrors' spread out from the original factory buildings;[5] some entrepreneurs were insensitive to old rights, for example, Arkwright as he 'intruded brusquely into the countryside' without first considering the interests of the Duke of Rutland.[6] The rich were able to buy their way into social approval; the less affluent found it more difficult. But neither was greatly inhibited by apparent lack of social status, and neither was faced by impenetrable social barriers. Wealth in England had always been as good as blood in opening doors; the industrial revolution made it even easier.

Can a balance sheet be drawn? In aggregate, yes. Since the industrial revolution did occur, obstacles to industrialization in eighteenth century England must have been surmounted or else must not have been powerful enough to have inhibited growth significantly. However, the listing and balancing of obstacles and inducements may not be as revealing as considering the general

---

[1] See the works of S. Pollard, E. J. Hobsbawm and E. P. Thompson.

[2] Mantoux, op. cit., pp. 403–8, for an account of the social status of the entrepreneurs.

[3] F. D. Klingender, *Art and the Industrial Revolution* (London, 1947), p. 93.

[4] Fitton and Wadsworth, op. cit., p. 97.

[5] Klingender, op. cit.

[6] E. L. Jones, 'Industrial Capital and Landed Investment: the Arkwrights in Herefordshire, 1809–43', *Land, Labour and Population in the Industrial Revolution*, ed. E. L. Jones and G. E. Mingay (London, 1967), p. 52.

social and economic maturity of England before the industrial revolution. If the presently accepted tests of economic backwardness are applied, the England of 1750 can be seen to be advanced rather than backward, so it is little surprise that entrepreneurs could thrive there. Taking H. Leibenstein's thirty-five characteristics of backwardness,[1] only six, and some of these doubtfully relevant, applied to eighteenth century England: of these six, three are demographic (high fertility and high mortality rates, rudimentary hygiene and public health), two are social (child labour and inferior status of women), and one technological (inadequate technical training). England before the industrial revolution was no backward country; rather it provided an environment in which enterprise could and did thrive.

[1] H. Leibenstein, *Economic Backwardness and Economic Growth* (New York, 1957), pp. 40-1.

3

E. L. JONES

English and European
Agricultural Development
1650-1750[1]

'I often met with it, that our Nation being much Exhausted and Ruined by
the Civil War, retrieved their great Losses by some new Husbandry, and in a
little time Recovered themselves and got to a better State than ever; but never
could learn what was this advantageous Improvement, till I found by Reading
Mr Hurtlib's Book of Husbandry, that it was principally by introducing this
Clover Grass, called Flanders Grass; because the Seed was bro't from Brabant
and other parts of Flanders.'

> Jared Eliot, quoted by C. R. Woodward
> *Ploughs and Politicks* (1941), 267, n.11.

There is a popular notion that depression obtained throughout
Europe between the early seventeenth century and the mid-
eighteenth century. Yet the supposed symptoms of such a
phenomenon—declining population, shrinking trade, social revolt
and agricultural recession—were present in less degree, or for
shorter intervals, or not at all, in England. Improvements in the
level, organization and method of production in England may
have been slight by later standards, but by contemporary standards
they were impressive. By about 1750 a little understood set of
circumstances had already placed England some way along the
road of economic growth. Famine was unlikely to threaten
seriously even the unprecedented growth of population which at
that date was imminent. Already England was richer than some
underdeveloped countries today. Moreover this success had come
during the otherwise widespread economic retardation which
ultimately encompassed even the precocious Dutch. A central

[1] I am indebted for valuable comments and discussion to L. E. Davis, C. M. Elliott,
R. M. Hartwell, J. R. T. Hughes and B. H. Slicher van Bath. This essay was written at
Purdue University, Indiana, in April 1966 and has since in no way been amended.

problem of the origins of industrialism is therefore to reconcile a 'general' depression during the seventeenth century and first half of the eighteenth century with the exceptional vigour of the English performance.[1]

In this essay on the agricultural sector I shall not contend that favourable developments within that sector were the sole or sufficient originators of economic growth. Nevertheless, its size within the whole economy was very large—approximately 68 per cent of families were engaged primarily in agriculture in 1688[2] —and its internal changes were likely to have wide significance. I shall suggest that English agriculture responded to a basically similar, if less intense, phase of low cereal prices between approximately 1650 and 1750 with more success than continental countries, and that this was a special help in putting the economy in an advantageous position for all-round growth during the eighteenth century. It will be seen that I do not regard the crucial developments in fodder cropping at this period, which underlay the expansion of agricultural output then and later, as consequent on population growth, as in Mrs Boserup's theory.[3] Instead, in her terms, I see them as the 'autonomous' responses of a particular agrarian structure and ecology to changing, and on the surface unfavourable, price levels for agricultural products.

I shall first consider the supposedly common characteristics of European agricultural depression during this hundred-year period; next, attempt to show that there was atypically vigorous activity in arable farming in England; then bring forward some factors which probably help to explain the divergence between England and continental countries in the mix, techniques and levels of their agricultural production; and finally, suggest some advantages which this may have imparted to mid-eighteenth century England. Admittedly, my explanatory sketches will be highly speculative. They require both integration in a more formal model of agricultural change in an economy at an early stage of development and much, much more effort at data-gathering. It is

---

[1] This has recently been pointed up in Trevor Aston (ed.), *Crisis in Europe 1560–1660: Essays from Past and Present 1952–62* (London, 1965), especially 'Introduction' by Christopher Hill and 'The Crisis of the Seventeenth Century, with a postscript', by E. J. Hobsbawm.

[2] Compared with 80 per cent in undeveloped countries and 15 per cent in many modern developed countries. Phyllis Deane, *The First Industrial Revolution* (Cambridge, 1965), p.13.

[3] Ester Boserup, *The Conditions of Agricultural Growth: The Economics of Agrarian Change under Population Pressure* (Chicago, 1965), 35–7.

precisely in order to attract fresh luminaries to longstanding pools of darkness, and to induce them to do work which is more consciously concerned with central issues of agricultural change than are many of the existing regional studies, that I offer this otherwise premature construct of late seventeenth and early eighteenth century agricultural development.

I

The author of the most comprehensive textbook on European agricultural history, Professor Slicher van Bath, depicts the period from the early seventeenth to the mid-eighteenth century as one of agricultural depression throughout western Europe, including England. More recently he has given us an important classification[1] of the recurrent features of agricultural expansions and contractions, based on the evidence previously collected in his *Agrarian History of Western Europe*. Within the period from the early seventeenth to the mid-eighteenth century he sees only the years of the War of the Spanish Succession as an aberrant spell of prosperity for arable farming. Flanking the secular contraction were the 'price revolution' of the sixteenth century and the rising price levels of the second half of the eighteenth century. The long, intervening depression was certainly far milder than the economic decline of the late Middle Ages, but in his scheme it displayed comparable symptoms. These stemmed primarily from falling cereal prices. In consequence, real incomes were high for the buyers of bread and low for landowners; there was little reclamation; ploughland was converted to pasture; the margin of cultivation retreated as tillage was abandoned; animal husbandry was expanded as a substitute; market gardening and the cultivation of industrial crops like flax, madder and hops, together with viticulture, were also expanded; and rural domestic industry, especially textile production, was developed to supplement low agricultural incomes. The central phenomenon was therefore the low exchange value of grain, which Professor Slicher is inclined to attribute mainly to demographic recession. Within generally weak agricultural activity there was some swing to livestock production, so that the characteristic feature of the period was an arable depression in western Europe.

[1] 'Les Problèmes Fondamentaux de la Société Préindustrielle en Europe Occidentale', *A. A. G. Bijdragen*, 12 (1965), pp. 5–46.

Professor Slicher's survey of the supporting evidence, drawn from an impressive range of national literatures, can be only briefly summarized here. Reclamation sank strikingly. In the Netherlands comparatively little fresh land was poldered between 1665 and 1764. In East Friesland, Germany, fen drainage came to a standstill for much of this time.

Table 1

WETLAND RECLAMATION IN EUROPE IN THE SEVENTEENTH
AND EIGHTEENTH CENTURIES

Area gained annually by poldering in the Netherlands and
by peat marsh reclamation in East Friesland, Germany

	Netherlands	Germany
1615–39	100	100
1640–64	56	84
1665–89	28	0
1690–1714	28	0
1715–39	24	17
1740–64	23	35
1765–89	40	77

Source: Redistributed figures from B. H. Slicher van Bath,
The Agrarian History of Western Europe (London,
1963), 200–203.

In Germany and Italy the margin of cultivation was actually on the retreat, some farms being abandoned. A slighter tendency towards similar misfortunes is adduced for English farms from Dr G. E. Mingay's paper on 'An Agricultural Depression 1730–1750',[1] but it is important for us to note that this article does refer only to the 1730s and '40s and that even then only the tiniest fraction of the Duke of Kingston's estates (which formed Dr Mingay's case study) became untenanted.

Where they were driven out of cereal farming by low prices many farmers switched over to livestock production. Ploughland was accordingly converted to grass in a number of countries. As an English illustration Professor Slicher mentions that Gabriel Plattes (d. 1644) had praised the Vale of Belvoir as the richest graingrowing land in Europe, whereas Defoe, at the start of the eighteenth century, was to laud the district as pasture and a famous nursery for horses and sheep. In the Netherlands farmers were turning to horticulture and the growing of industrial crops and were establishing tree nurseries or planting bulbs. Viticulture was spreading in southern France, Catalonia and Switzerland.

[1] Economic History Review, 2nd ser. VIII (1956), pp. 323–38.

Real wages do seem to have been generally high for the buyers of bread, although this fortunate situation was interrupted on the continent from time to time by bouts of famine.[1] These periodic famines among years of plenty suggest that there was insufficient improvement in continental farming techniques to reduce the impact on the harvest of intermittently adverse weather conditions. Professor Slicher, however, is able to cite complaints from France, Germany and England that labourers fared better than their masters, for wages were sticky while, in most years, food (and farm product) prices were sinking. Examples from Twente (Netherlands), Westphalia, Switzerland, Scotland and Ireland (to which Picardy may be added[2]) are also cited to show that textile industries were being developed in order to offset poor returns from farming and to employ those who could no longer find a living on the land. This process was seemingly only reversed after 1750, by a switch of population back into agriculture, when at one and the same time higher cereal prices distressed the weavers and made farming more attractive, and when competition from English factory-made cottons damaged European domestic and small town linen producers. In eastern Europe meanwhile there was an extension of the serf-farmed estates of the great magnates. Grain from that region largely captured the abnormally urban and industrial market of the Netherlands. The ability of eastern European agriculture to supply cheap cereals to the west even during the 'depression' depended, however, on the extensive cultivation of new lands by a serf population and not on the fruitful new technology which this essay will attempt to show was achieved in England.

The continental western European country in which falling cereal prices seemed initially, at any rate, to be least damaging was the Netherlands. Cheap, imported foodstuffs seem to have released Dutch resources for more productive activities than growing cereals. Since the Netherlands constituted England's main commercial and industrial rival it is worth looking a little more closely at her experience. Certainly population and cereal prices fell more seriously there than in England.[3] Records of the Dutch drainage administrations show how sharp was the

---

[1] Cf. Pierre Goubert, 'The French Peasantry of the Seventeenth Century: A Regional Example', *Past and Present*, 10 (1956), pp. 66, 69–70, 74.

[2] Ibid., p. 61.

[3] J. A. Faber et al., 'Population changes and economic developments in the Netherlands: a historical survey', *A. A. G. Bijdragen*, 12 (1956), pp. 47–113.

contraction in poldering activity. A special difficulty in western Holland was that were cultivation to be continued at all, the dykes simply had to be maintained. The fixed charges for this probably imposed a proportionately heavier burden at a time when farm product prices were falling.

Productive investment in Dutch agriculture appears to have been cut back. During the sixteenth and early seventeenth centuries merchants, mainly Amsterdammers, had put money into land, buying estates which had both tenanted farms and summer houses for the merchants' own families. During the first half of the seventeenth century they spent enthusiastically on reclamation projects. Early maps show North Holland literally taking shape at this time from amidst a maze of lagoons. Between 1597 and 1635 the Zijpe and Wieringerwaard were diked, and the Beemster, Zoetermeer, Purmer, 's-Gravenland and some smaller meres were drained. Dutch money, again predominantly from Amsterdam, even helped to drain marshes in France, as well as the Isle of Axholme, Canvey Island, Hatfield Chase and the Great Level of the Fens in England. But about 1650, when agriculture became less profitable, there was a rapid and strictly business-like retraction. For example, the one hundred or so Amsterdam merchants who had earlier financed the reclamation of the Beemster Meer in North Holland (costing f. 1,492,500 between 1608–12) and who owned estates there, rid themselves of their land and returned abruptly to the city.[1] Commercial opportunities were clearly superior in the Netherlands. Although after this the Dutch were sometimes prone to squander capital in investment 'bubbles' (like the tulip manias of the 1680s and following the Peace of Utrecht) they were not again tempted to sink any surplus funds in farming and probably not again in overseas temperate agriculture until the American ventures of the Holland Land Company at the end of the eighteenth century. They became instead big food importers, regularly bringing 20,000 to 30,000 lean beeves from Jutland and Holstein to fatten on the polders of Holland, and buying up French cereals before the harvest, wines before the vintage and so much brandy that the *bruleries* caused a wood shortage.[2] Even

[1] Violet Barbour, *Capitalism in Amsterdam in the 17th Century* (Ann Arbor, 1963), pp. 28, 60–1, 120–2. In Denmark, too, landed property ceased to attract investment: 'Here the Courtier buys no Land, but remits his Money to the Bank of Amsterdam, or of Hamburg ... few or none of them (the Ministers of State) purchase any Lands, but place their Money in the Banks of Amsterdam and Hamburg.' (Barbour, 46–7, quoting Robert Molesworth in 1694.)
[2] Ibid. pp. 91–2.

more, they brought large quantities of grain from the extensive agricultures of the Baltic countries and even from East Anglia. The Dutch were thus substituting cheaper cereals for their own production. Sir William Petty noted the concentration by the Dutchmen on dairying and feeding cattle for dung to fertilize rape, flax and madder crops, 'wherefore there is little Ploughing, and Sowing of Corn in *Holland* and *Zealand*, or breeding of young Cattle.'[1] He repeated later that, 'the other Trade of which the *Hollanders* have rid their Hands, is the old Patriarchal Trade of being Cow-keepers, and in a great Measure of that which concerns Ploughing and Sowing of Corn, having put that Employment upon the *Danes* and *Polanders*, from whom they have their Young Cattle and Corn.'[2] But what is more curious is that the English, hitherto slight net importers, were now producing grain cheaply enough to join the ranks of the exporters. How had this come about?

II

Indeed, the more general question is raised of how far English agricultural experience really did conform to the wider west European pattern of depression. The prevailing view is still that the period before 1750 saw only the most sluggish advance in English agriculture. Professor Slicher believes that England experienced depression akin to that in mainland Europe. Mrs Thirsk has claimed that 'the low price for agricultural produce... held back the enterprising farmer in the first half of the [eighteenth] century.'[3] Professor Habakkuk, in a passage quoted approvingly by Miss Deane and Dr Cole, states that, 'the low or stationary agricultural prices of the earlier decades of the [eighteenth] century had a depressing effect on agricultural investment... the rising prices over most of the second half of the century stimulated agricultural investment.'[4] Recently Mrs Mitchison has held that despite depression in English agriculture,

[1] C. H. Hull (ed.), *The Economic Writings of Sir William Petty*, I (Cambridge, 1899), p. 259 (from the *Political Arithmetick* of 1676).
[2] Ibid., p. 267. See also Cantillon, quoted by Mogens Boserup, 'Agrarian Structure and Take-off', in W. W. Rostow (ed.), *The Economics of Take-off into Sustained Growth* (London, 1963), p. 202 n.1.
[3] *English Peasant Farming* (London, 1957), pp. 205–6.
[4] 'The Eighteenth Century', *Econ. Hist. Rev.* 2nd ser. VIII (1956), 437–8, quoted in *British Economic Growth 1688–1959* (Cambridge, 1962), p. 90.

'progress was intermittently made in agricultural improvement', but she does not spell out the supposed periodicity.[1] Another recent contributor, Professor Charles Wilson, while admitting that some innovation took place, emphasizes 'how small was the influence of the new ideas statistically',[2] although since he bases this view on figures of the area under turnips which he does not supply and for which he gives no source, and on Mr Fussell's calculations about the small import of clover seed from the Low Countries, it is most unconvincing. The clover seed calculation supposes that imported seed at the end of the seventeenth century was sufficient to sow only one in every 580 cultivated acres, which is said to mean that only 16,000 acres could have been cultivated under the Norfolk four-course rotation. This is misleading. Clover was almost certainly more widely grown in loose rotations in the south and west than in East Anglia under the strict four-course. Furthermore, clover had been present for half a century, ample time to develop home seed production since the plant is perennial and will seed profusely wherever (in the case of broad clover) the aftermath is left to flower. Seed: yield ratios are as high as 1 : 25, so that even if only a few farmers had grown seed, home output in any one year was likely to exceed imports substantially. Indeed, the price of seed was falling, from over one shilling per lb. before 1655 to 3d. or less by 1690. The imports were probably just a convenient backload for Dutch merchants settled in England to export English woollens. We know that those on the Strand at Topsham in Devon distributed clover seed throughout the south-west.[3]

Most writers thus still minimize the extent of new cropping practices in English agriculture before 1750, although perhaps with less confidence of late. This habit of playing down technical change before the mid-eighteenth century and conversely exaggerating its novelty in the second half of that century has a long history, which necessarily means that the customary view will not dislodge easily. In the historiography of the subject there has admittedly been an intervening phase when the advances of the

---

[1] Rosalind Mitchison, 'The Movements of Scottish Corn Prices in the Seventeenth and Eighteenth Centuries', *Econ. Hist. Rev.* 2nd ser. XVIII (1965), p. 291.

[2] Charles Wilson, *England's Apprenticeship 1603–1763* (London, 1965), p. 145. England and the Netherlands were already exchanging the seed of various industrial crops in the early seventeenth century.

[3] Charles Wilson, *Holland and Britain* (London, n.d.), p. 108.

early eighteenth century were fully recognized,[1] but this recognition faded again, perhaps because the most prominent agricultural publicist of the early eighteenth century, Jethro Tull, was fairly readily dismissed as a crank of no great practical influence. It should, however, be observed that those who stress the achievements of late eighteenth century England tend to lean heavily on Arthur Young's incessant axe-grinding journalism, on over-emphasizing the spread and merit of the Norfolk rotation, and on too ready an acceptance of Parliamentary enclosure as a source and measure of technical progress and rising output.

Surprisingly, modern writers often seem less cautious about throwing the weight of change onto the late eighteenth century than was the first historian to articulate the history of the so-called industrial and agricultural revolutions, Arnold Toynbee.[2] Scrutinized, Toynbee's remarks on agriculture reveal internal conflict. Too scrupulous to suppress evidence contrary to his theme that economic change occurred dramatically after 1760, but nevertheless over-committed to this thesis, he tried to qualify and explain away the evidence he had unearthed of substantial technical progress before that date. In so doing Toynbee was exercizing the historian's art of weaving fragments of data into a consistent tale. In a discipline so overlain with literary ambitions as economic history is (or was) that temptation is admittedly difficult to avoid— if, with such scrappy evidence as survives, any tale is to be told with effect. Toynbee certainly more than half convinced himself that in 1760 agricultural improvements remained limited to a few localities; he produced what has since become the standard myth of the technical primacy of Norfolk; he cited Arthur Young's claim that 1700–1760 were years of stagnation owing to low prices, something which Young himself contradicted elsewhere, at least for Norfolk;[3] and Toynbee declared that before 1760 there was little progress in livestock breeding, despite himself citing inherently more plausible efforts to upgrade sheep breeds at least as early as the 1730s.

The important point is that Toynbee realized that 'the evidence on some points is somewhat contradictory' and that local studies

---

[1] See, e.g., D. G. Barnes, *A History of the English Corn Laws from 1660–1846* (London, 1930), p. 29.
[2] *Lectures on the Industrial Revolution of the 18th Century in England* (New York, n.d.), pp. 41–5.
[3] Cf. footnote 6 on p. 59.

published since his day clearly indicate considerable technical change before 1750. Toynbee admitted that, 'in spite of the ignorance and stupidity[sic] of the farmers and their use of wretched implements, the average produce of wheat was large'. He showed that progress in fodder cropping (particularly the growing of turnips to feed lean sheep)[1] had been made throughout southern England by the mid-eighteenth century, some of it certainly in the late seventeenth century—but he then went on to play this down with the inaccurate and irrelevant remark that only in Norfolk were turnips fed to cattle. But he did concede that clover husbandry was 'universal from the North of England to the further end of Glamorganshire.'

Subsequently, as has been shown, many historians have been inclined to ignore or belittle the achievements of the pre-1750 period. If we pick the most famous cropping innovation, the introduction of the turnip as a field crop, and contemplate the sources on which successive investigators have too often placed great reliance, the origin of their partiality towards the late eighteenth century becomes clear. The core sources are the *General Views* of the agriculture of each county, written in the 1790s and 1800s by Arthur Young and his circle. Comments on the introduction of the turnip by these contemporaries prove to be couched in the vaguest terms: 'increase very great', 'but recently introduced', 'considerable quantities', 'extended application' and so forth. They do not even succeed in throwing light on the history of the crop during the second quarter of the century, which after all was only at the edge of living memory. Neither had the authors of the *General Views* customarily consulted such early writers as Ellis, Lisle, Houghton or Mortimer, a shortcoming which helps to explain their more blatant inaccuracies. Young, for instance, credited Jethro Tull with the first introduction of turnips to England, while Nathaniel Kent claimed that Townshend had first introduced them into Norfolk.[2] Boys proclaimed that in Kent 'thirty years previously [i.e. about 1765] hardly one farmer in a hundred grew any'[3] although we know that they

---

[1] 'Of late years there have been improvements made in the breed of sheep by changing of rams and sowing of turnips and grass seeds, and now there is some large fine combing wool to be found in most counties in England.' Quoted from *Pamphlet by a Woollen Manufacturer of Northampton*, 1739.

[2] Arthur Young, *Six Weeks' Tour* (1769), ix; Nathaniel Kent, *General View . . . Norfolk* (1796), p. 40.

[3] John Boys, *General View . . . Kent* (1796), p. 92.

were introduced at Godington as early as 1685 and according to Kalm were being grown commonly at Gravesend and elsewhere by 1748, while Young himself attested to their general use in 1770.[1] Young's calculation that the cultivation of turnips in east Hampshire expanded twenty-fold in the dozen years before 1769 is also open to doubt in view of plentiful earlier evidence, as is William Pitt's statement that about 1774 turnips were 'scarcely at all known' in Staffordshire.[2] Robert Lowe, the Nottinghamshire man who compiled the *General View* of 1798 for that county, went so far as to claim that the introduction of turnips and seeds [clover, etc.], 'is scarce so old in this Kingdom as the beginning of this century, and much later in this country', whereas in reality in his own county farmers were protesting in 1707–08 that the Sherwood Forest deer were consuming their turnips in the fields, while clover was being grown there at least as early as 1692.[3] Reliance, at base, on the *General Views* must unavoidably assign crucial husbandry innovations to impossibly late dates. Sources which have a built-in tendency to attribute cropping innovations to the late eighteenth century mis-date the spread of the turnip, and since this was undoubtedly a laggard among the 'new' fodder crops must even more seriously mis-date the spread of clover, sainfoin and so forth. It is not enough for present-day writers to acknowledge the earlier introduction of these crops, of which more and more evidence is being published, only to dismiss them at once as mere exceptions.

This prolonged digression has been pursued in order to cast doubt on the conventional picture of significant agricultural innovation only after 1750. This essay is not an attempt to contend that English agriculture wholly evaded the earlier consequences of poor prices, since clearly it did not. If England was unique in the scale of her innovation before that date, in other respects her agricultural condition and that of western Europe were superficially similar. 'Times with farmers grow worse and worse' wrote a Hertfordshire agriculturist to his brother in London in 1738 or '39,[4]

<hr/>

[1] J. Lucas (transl.), *Pehr Kalm—Account of his visit to England* (1892), p. 441 and passim; Arthur Young, *Eastern Tour* (1771, III, pp. 1–17).

[2] *Six Weeks' Tour*, p. 214; William Pitt, *General View . . . Staffs.* (1808), p. 313ff.

[3] *General View . . . Notts.* (1798), p. 167. Cf. J. D. Chambers, 'The Problem of Sherwood Forest', *Agriculture*, LXII (1955), p. 178, and A. H. John, 'Aspects of English Economic Growth in the first half of the Eighteenth Century', *Economica*, N.S. XXVIII (1961), p. 179.

[4] Delmé Radcliffe Collection, Hertfordshire Record Office: DE 4659.

during one of the intermittent spells of agrarian distress.[1] English price experience was not unlike that of the continent, with the qualification that the fall in the price of wheat was weaker, later to develop and less sustained. The evidence is, however, that stronger counteracting tendencies were evident in England than in mainland Europe, tendencies which appear to explain both the cushioned impact of the price fall and the structure of the agriculture which emerged in England so conveniently in time for the late eighteenth century swelling of population.

Table 2

PRICE INDICES FOR WHEAT IN WESTERN EUROPE
1601–1800

	1601/50	1651/1700	1701/50	1751/1800
Northern Italy	210	113	103	145
France	159	140	113	135
Amsterdam	146	103	109	143
England	124	126	106	143

Source: Slicher van Bath, op. cit. 326–7, derived from various national publications. Figures rounded to nearest whole number. 1721–45 = 100.

Symptoms of an agricultural 'contraction', similar to those in Professor Slicher's scheme, do seem to have been forthcoming in England, but they were oddly muffled or incomplete. It is worth reviewing them in order to underline this interpretation. There were, for instance, conversions of arable land to pasture. However, on closer consideration these seem to have been essentially the grassing down of heavier land (like the Vale of Belvoir, mentioned above) which could no longer compete with the spread of cereal cultivation on more cheaply tilled light soils, now being brought into permanent cultivation on a wide scale. In other words, the conversions to pasture were one face of a process of regional adjustment within English agriculture (discussed below) and not a sign of the 'expected' net switch into pasture farming. It was in the clay vales and the Midlands, worst hit by the impoverishment of small, heavy land, grain growers in a time of weak prices, and hence turning over to the less labour-intensive

[1] See G. E. Mingay, *English Landed Society in the Eighteenth Century* (London, 1963), pp. 54–5.

production of stock, that domestic industries like framework knitting caught on at this time. The rise of supplementary or alternative occupations to agriculture was localized, not universal.

There is evidence of the 'expected' expansion of livestock populations, mainly, however, of sheep, which *via* the manuring and treading of light soils under the sheep-fold were destined to play a key role in the extension of cereal production at this time. There were signs, too, of more market gardening, orcharding and the growing of industrial crops like hops and flax. But despite some efforts by the Herefordshire gentry, viticulture did not regain a hold in England, while the growing of tobacco, which was forming a substitute for unprofitable cereal growing in the Veluwve (Netherlands), was restricted in England chiefly to parts of Gloucestershire and Wiltshire, and finally in 1672 prohibited in order to protect distressed colonial producers. This suppression of tobacco growing in England blocked an alternative to cereal production which was open to European farmers. Lastly, it does seem true to say that the period was one of high real wages. Cheap grain for the brewers and distillers, and the extension of cider apple orchards in Devon and Hereford, gave rise to the inebriated England of Hogarth's Gin Lane.

III

Where England conclusively stood apart from her neighbours was in a higher level of activity in arable farming, particularly the accession of land to the tillage area by various forms of reclamation. In 1662 John Evelyn protested at 'the impolitic diminution of our timber . . . from the disproportionate spreading of tillage' as those who had bought estates during the Commonwealth razed the trees from them.[1] There are difficulties in measuring this and subsequent extensions of cultivation. We cannot use the rate of enclosure by Acts of parliament as an indicator (although something of the sort is often implied in the literature) because enclosure, let alone Parliamentary enclosure, is not synonymous with reclamation. Reliance on the movements of enclosure Acts—simply because there are figures—grossly underrates the earlier and continuing processes of enclosure by

[1] In *Sylva* (York, 1782), I, pp. 1–2, first presented to the Royal Society in 1662. Quoted in R. G. Albion, *Forests and Sea Power* (Cambridge, Mass., 1926), p. 131.

private agreement, and ignores the more definitely productive extensions of the cultivated area by the reclamation of privately-owned rough pasture. Formal enclosure processes did not necessarily bring about increases in output, and in practice many such enclosures may merely have redistributed land without for some time changing much else. Certainly enclosure was neither consistently a physical nor a financial success. In the Vale of Pickering William Marshall noted that 'many men of comfortable fortunes have in this district been beggared and the fortunes of others injured by the inclosing of land which have not yet paid',[1] while in Hampshire he saw abandoned enclosures on some hillsides, just as in the early nineteenth century others were to see Otmoor in Oxfordshire (which had been enclosed so ruthlessly) resist reclamation. Another indicator of arable expansion might be the progress of marsh and fen reclamation, but here England lacks figures of the acreages drained comparable with those for Holland and Germany. We are left without exact statistical measures of the extension of the arable area and are thrown back on the unfashionable picking and scratching of the local historian.

The reconstruction of the phases of the piecemeal extension of cultivation from scattered and incomplete documents is tedious; the available records will never permit the building of an exact chronology. Nevertheless, enough fragments of evidence can be assembled to show that far from being as elsewhere in western Europe a period of generally retreating cultivation, the century after 1650 was in England one of considerable addition to the arable acreage. Some of this was in the Royal Forests which became available to cultivators with the collapse of the monarchy. In Northamptonshire and Bedfordshire new land was provided during the second half of the seventeenth century by the disparking and turning to cultivation of royal parks, on a sufficient scale to provoke a shortage of substantial tenant farmers.[2] Rather more land was reclaimed in the fens and marshes, by moneyed men anticipating a profit on an increased output of agricultural produce for the market.[3] But it must not be pretended that compared with

---

[1] *Rural Economy of Yorkshire* (1788), I, p. 84, quoted by Brian Loughborough in *Agric. Hist. Rev.* XIII (1965), p. 111.
[2] H. J. Habakkuk, 'English Landownership, 1680–1740', *Econ. Hist. Rev.* X (1940), p. 14.
[3] For example, the drainage of Bedford Level entered a new stage of activity in 1685; Thomas Fleetwood drained Marton Mere in Lancashire in the 1690s; twenty years later

Footnote continued on page 56.

earlier or later periods this hundred years saw an impressive reclamation of wetlands. The big arable 'push' was destined to take place not there but on the free-draining uplands.

More diffuse, but in area much more significant, was indeed the extension of tillage by the breaking-up of sheep pastures on the dry downs and wolds. This was a laborious task involving paring off the turf with a breast-plough, and heaping up the sods for burning, but it was cheaper than draining marshes and keeping up dykes and outfalls which was the only way if new land were to be inned, say, in East Friesland or the Netherlands. Big inroads into the sheep pastures were made in this hundred years. 'Doth a man plow upon the rocks?' asked a Nonconformist minister when he saw grain waving for the first time on the chalk slopes of the Yorkshire wolds in 1666.[1] Aubrey and Defoe both commented on the large scale conversion of sheep-down to ploughland in the central mass of the southern chalk, the Salisbury Plain area. Defoe noted the practice of intensive sheep folding—'a new method of husbandry'—which was enabling good crops of wheat and barley to be taken from the thin chalk soils, and he reported that with this aid a great part of the chalk throughout Hampshire, Wiltshire and Dorset was being brought into cultivation.[2] The dung of sheep fed on the introduced fodder crops kept up soil fertility and made it possible for the first time to keep vast expanses of the chalklands permanently under crops.

Summaries of further evidence relating to the chalklands[3] show that there was considerable activity in ploughing downland from

Footnote continued from page 55

John Perry stopped the Dagenham breach on the Thames and reclaimed about 5,000 acres; Lindsay Level was taken in hand. G. N. Clark, *The Wealth of England* (London, 1946), p. 153. Of Romney Marsh it was said in 1719 that there had been an 'abundance of land gained from the sea, and inned' since 1657. C. W. Chalklin, *Seventeenth Century Kent* (London, 1965), p. 15. In 1670 John Evelyn arrived at Soham meres in Cambridgeshire to find Lord Wotton and Sir Jan Kiviet, 'about their draining Engines, having it seems undertaken to do wonders, on a vast piece of Marchground [marsh], they had hired of Sir Tho: Chichley.' E. S. de Beer (ed.), *The Diary of John Evelyn* (Oxford, 1955), III, p. 555 and n. 3. Kiviet was a Dutchman who had fled to England for political reasons and is not symptomatic of a renewed flow of Dutch capital into English drainage schemes. Finally, in 1675 at Wawne in the Hull valley in Yorkshire, windmills were erected to pump off water and the newly-drained carrs were sown to rape and oats. Alan Harris, *The Rural Landscape of the East Riding of Yorkshire 1700–1850* (London, 1961), p. 36.

[1] Clark, op. cit., p. 153.

[2] Daniel Defoe, *A Tour through England and Wales* (London, Everyman edition, 1928), I, pp. 187, 285.

[3] E. L. Jones, 'Eighteenth-Century Changes in Hampshire Chalkland Farming', *Agric. Hist. Rev.* VIII (1960), pp. 8, 12–13; M. C. Naish, *The Agricultural Landscape of the Hampshire Chalklands 1700–1840*, London M.A. thesis, 1960, passim, especially pp. 157–8.

the late seventeenth century until about 1750, a relative quietus during the third quarter of the eighteenth century (despite rising cereal prices), and another surge of cultivation after 1775. This agrees quite well with the periodicity of agricultural improvement in Norfolk. Additional data now to hand from a survey of the eighteenth-century farm accounts available in the record offices of almost all the southern counties[1] confirm that the first half of the century, even the 'depression' of the years 1730–50, was far from a typical 'contraction'; cultivation continued to be extended widely. At Stoke Charity, Hampshire, downland was broken up in 1726, so that the output of wheat rose sharply in 1727 (the tithes rose from 42 quarters 5 bushels to 101½ quarters).[2] In King's Somborne parish, Hampshire, in the late 1720s much land was broken up, for example in 1729 Marsh Hill was ploughed and put into a wheat/barley/two years' seeds rotation. In 1735 one hundred acres of 'first bake' (land of which the turf had been pared-and-burnt prior to cultivation) was to be enclosed and kept sown in course under a private enclosure agreement relating to the adjacent parish of Broughton.[3] Broughton Common Down was broken up in 1735 and '36.[4] During the 1730s there was grubbing and enclosing on Southam Motts Holmwood Farm, Chailey, Kent.[5] Between 1738–41 there was extensive grubbing and ditching on a farm in hand in the Guildford area of Surrey.[6] At Castle Farm, East Lulworth, Dorset, between 1738 and 1745 several small acreages of land were brought into cultivation by grubbing.[7] Part of Compton Down in Hampshire was burn-baked and converted to tillage in 1741.[8] At Moreton Farm in Dorset two hundred acres of wood and down were 'enclosed divided and converted to tillage' in 1743, while in 1744 one hundred and forty acres of heathland on Moreton Common were enclosed by private agreement.[9] There was also extensive Devon-shiring (paring-and-burning) on Tatlingbury Farm near Tudely in Kent between 1745 and 1753.[10] Especially during the 1740s, a great

[1] Part of a Nuffield College research project carried out by E. J. T. Collins and the writer.
[2] Account of Joshua Reynolds, 1718–28, Corpus Christi College Library, Oxford.
[3] Hampshire Record Office, Gatehouse Collection: 35M63/7.
[4] Nottingham University Archives, Manvers Collection, Rentals 4344–48, 4509–48.
[5] E. Sussex R.O. Additional Mss. 4461.
[6] Staffs. R.O. Dyott Coll. D661/8/1/22.
[7] Dorset R.O. D/10/68.
[8] Hampshire R.O. 18m54/F.1 and Box H pkt. F, No. 15.
[9] Dorset R.O. D29/E28.
[10] Farm account in the Rothamsted Collection.

deal of liming and ditching was carried out on many farms. To these examples may be added the evidence of the process of persistent nibbling whereby numbers of new, small farms and fields were being hedged, pared-and-burnt or 'Devonshired', and limed and dunged on the Devon moorland throughout the second half of the seventeenth century and the early eighteenth century, as indeed at other periods.[1]

Together with the evidence summarized in earlier work, these examples show that there was a fairly strong tide of reclamation during the late seventeenth century and the first half of the eighteenth century, and further that this was by no means at its lowest ebb during the most difficult years of the 1730s and '40s. There does not seem to have been that slump in reclamation, abandonment of arable land and conversion of ploughland to pasture which is theoretically to be anticipated of a 'contraction'. Admittedly there was some offsetting grassing-down of heavy clayland in England at this period. We know too little of the magnitudes to be certain, but it is highly unlikely that this counter-movement involved as great an acreage as that which was freshly taken into tillage. The probability was therefore that the net cereal acreage tended to grow, and that the total output of grain consequently edged up. Even had the reclamation movement and the conversion of clayland to pasture entirely cancelled out, the English experience was that there was a marked extension of cultivation on the light-soiled uplands, a shift, that is, in the locus of arable farming away from the clay vales. This in itself would require explanation. Such a movement is not comprehended in Professor Slicher's scheme, nor apparently were similar inversions to be found on the continent.

A second respect in which England differed from Europe, as has been indicated earlier, was in the vigour of her agricultural innovation during the hundred years in question. Before the middle of the seventeenth century change was slow; contemporaries were definite that new husbandry practices rather suddenly became acceptable to the landed interest during and immediately after the Civil War-Interregnum period. Until the middle of the seventeenth century, according to John Aubrey, 'twas held a strange presumption for a Man to attempt an

---

[1] W. G. Hoskins, 'The Reclamation of the Waste in Devon, 1550–1800', *Econ. Hist. Rev.* XIII (1943), especially pp. 90–1.

Innovation in Learning . . . even to attempt an improvement in Husbandry (though it succeeded with profit) was look'd upon with an ill Eie. Their Neighbours did scorne to follow it, though not to doe it, was to their own Detriment.'[1] Charles Davenant noted that clover had been introduced during the Interregnum, especially on Crown lands.[2] John Houghton referred to 'the great improvements made of lands since our inhuman civil wars, when our gentry, who before hardly knew what it was to think, then fell to such an industry and caused such an improvement, as England never knew before.'[3] The new interest is revealed by the investigation into farming practices which the Royal Society undertook soon after the Restoration; Houghton specifically attributed much of the innovation after 1660 to the fact that, 'the whole land hath been fermented and stirred up by the profitable hints it hath received from the Royal Society.'[4] Aubrey agreed, only setting the change at about 1649, when the Royal Society's immediate predecessor, the Experimental Philosophy Club at Oxford, started up.[5] In the course of the Nuffield College study it was found that innumerable manuscript and published sources confirmed the middle decades of the seventeenth century as a very significant period for innovation. This was the time when the turnip emerged from gardens and became a field crop, when clover, sainfoin and ryegrass were first widely cultivated, and when floated water meadows (i.e. irrigated pastures) were being energetically engineered. From then on, through the years 1650–1750, all these novelties penetrated far into English agriculture; turnips admittedly lagged rather, but made a stronger appearance in the low price period of the 1740s. The degree of acceptance of these crops and practices is truly surprising in view of the custom of assigning major innovation to the second half of the eighteenth century. Yet Arthur Young had observed of Norfolk that 'for 30 years from 1730 to 1760, the great improvements of the north western part of the county took place . . . For the next 30 years to about 1790 they nearly stood still; they *reposed upon their laurels*.'[6]

The primary effect of these innovations was to provide a much

[1] Oliver Lawson Dick, *Aubrey's Brief Lives* (London, 1950), xlii.
[2] Cited by Christopher Hill, *The Century of Revolution 1603–1714* (Edinburgh, 1961), p. 150.
[3] R. Bradley (ed.), *Husbandry and Trade Improv'd: [by] John Houghton* (1727), p. 56.
[4] Quoted by Wilson, op. cit., p. 145.
[5] Lawson Dick, op. cit., xlii.
[6] Arthur Young, *General View . . . Norfolk* (1804), p. 31.

greater supply of fodder. As early as about 1673 Aubrey noted that in the Elsted district of Surrey 'clover grass has reduced the price of meadow hay from £3 to £1 per load.'[1] John Worlidge claimed in 1687 that the success of the 'new' grasses had been 'the occasion of the many endeavours that were used by some Northern Graziers to obtain a law to suppress the Improvements in the Southern Parts, lest Grass and Grazing Grounds should become as plentiful in these as in other parts.'[2] William Ellis, too, had heard that about the late 1680s the men of the Vale of Aylesbury, 'strove with great might to suppress the sowing of the [clover] in the Chilterns or hilly Country.' They failed, but in Ellis's view were not unwise to have tried, since neither clover nor turnips did well in the deep, heavy soils of their open fields in the Vale, while one acre of clover grown on the hills could feed as many cattle as three acres of the Vale's permanent pasture. The innovations, concentrated on the uplands, were a threat to the economic position of the heavy land farmers, who must formerly have agisted beasts for their Chiltern neighbours, and indeed the price of permanent meadow fell in many places.[3] These attempts at the legal suppression of the new fodder crops during the 1680s are interesting in that they doubtless mark an outstanding phase of innovation, and one which was perhaps active during the spell of falling wheat prices of that decade.

Hitherto, shortages of animal feedstuffs had been a constraint on agricultural production, especially in the dry chalk or limestone uplands and the sandlands—areas that benefited most from the new forage crops and (in the former case) from floated meadow. Now that fodder shortages were being overcome, a barrier to higher production was lifted. Given a constant or increasing head of stock (and the signs are of growth, especially in sheep numbers) more feed would mean a greater production of dung with which to raise yields on the arable land, the area of which, as we saw earlier, was almost certainly expanding. Clearly, some of the existing cultivated land must have been turned over to fodder crops but this would have been in its

---

[1] Quoted by William Marshall, *Review of the Southern and Peninsular Departments of England* (1817). A Dorset farmer observed in 1760 that because of improved sources of fodder (notably clover) the value of water meadow had actually fallen since 1700. Dorset R.O. D/29E68.
[2] *Systema Agriculturae* London (1687), p. 26. Not in the 1668–9 edition.
[3] William Ellis, *The Practical Farmer* (1732), pp. 41–2, 48, 53.

formerly unproductive fallow spell. Admittedly, it might be tempting to write off the changes of the period as a switch into livestock production when relative prices favoured this, particularly in the second quarter of the eighteenth century. Yet the additional dung from more and better-fed stock together with an actual increase in the cultivated area, on which would be grown cereals as well as forage crops (including the new legumes which directly improved soil fertility) suggests a rise in the physical output of both cereals and livestock.

Contemporary Englishmen agreed that output had risen. Houghton observed that 'parks have been disparked, commons inclosed, woods turned into arable, and pasture land improved by clover, st. foine, turnips, coleseed, parsley, and many other good husbandries, so that the food of cattle is increased as fast if not faster than the consumption, and by these means, although some particular lands may fall, I strongly persuade myself that altogether the rent of the kingdom is far greater than ever it was.'[1] According to Petty, England 'doth so abound in Laws against the Importation of *Cattle*, *Flesh* and *Fish* from abroad; and that the draining of *Fens*, improving of *Forests*, inclosing of *Commons*, Sowing of *St. Foyne* and *Clovergrass*, be grumbled against by Landlords, as the Way to depress the price of Victuals.'[2] And again, 'it is manifest [for a similar list of reasons] that the Land in its present Condition, is able to bear more Provision, and Commodities, than it was forty years ago.[3] Exports greatly increased, although consecutive figures to illustrate this survive only from 1697.

Table 3

NET EXPORT OF WHEAT, WHEATEN FLOUR, BARLEY,
OATS AND MALT FROM GREAT BRITAIN, 1700–49
(in thousands of quarters)

1700/09	1100
1710/19	1134
1720/29	1071
1730/39	3039
1740/49	3008

Source: B. R. Mitchell and Phyllis Deane, *Abstract of British Historical Statistics* (Cambridge, 1962), 94, 96.

[1] Quoted by Wilson, op. cit., p. 145.
[2] Hull, op. cit., pp. 287–8.
[3] Ibid., p. 303.

Apart from the 1690s the period 1650–1750 was, therefore, generally one of adequate or plentiful foodstuffs; it is true that there were occasions when the poor still rose up against the wagons and barges of the grain exporters[1] but the timing of such affrays shows them to have been brought about more by fearful anticipation than by repeated realities of famine. Starvation was apparently very rare in England. 'Crises of subsistence' such as disrupted parts of France were absent. We have to account for this agricultural good fortune in England and (although it is treacherous without more continental information) to explain how the country was able to develop viable mixed farming systems at this period when the continent did not.

IV

Firstly, England has the advantages of an island situation, advantages of which contemporaries (and Shakespeare before them) were well aware.[2] She was spared or lashed only by the tail of the ravages of continental wars, epidemics, and arbitrary taxations like those of German princelings striving to emulate the splendours of Versailles. The large oppressed minority of farmers from the Rhinish Palatinate who fled to America at the start of the eighteenth century to become the Pennsylvania Dutch seem to have had no real English equivalents, indeed it was to the Rhine-landers that the British government looked for ready hands to produce naval stores in the American colonies.[3] Admittedly the Rhinelanders had contemporary Irish counterparts, but then Irish agriculture was disrupted by religious persecution and systematic rack-renting by English landlords in the first half of the eighteenth century.[4]

Britain's end-of-the line position was especially advantageous in minimizing the effect of the cattle plagues which swept out of the mysterious and insanitary Orient in the 1710s and 1740s and '50s. English losses on the highest guesstimate were only a tiny

[1] Barnes, op. cit., pp. 13, 22.

[2] A contemporary account of these advantages is given in J. H. Hollander (ed.), *Nicholas Barbon on a Discourse of Trade 1690* (Baltimore, 1903), p. 31. Cf. John of Gaunt in *Richard II*, Act. II, Sc. 1, 'this fortress built by nature for herself against infection and the hand of war.'

[3] W. A. Knittle, *Early Eighteenth Century Palatine Emigration* (Philadelphia, 1937), pp. 3–5, 12.

[4] W. F. Dunaway, *The Scotch-Irish of Colonial Pennsylvania* (London, 1962), pp. 29–31.

fraction of the annual kill, whereas in the Netherlands, at the other extreme, over 70 per cent of the cattle population succumbed in the first year of attack. Countries with strong central governments were able to enforce the slaughter of infected beasts, but the loose association of the Dutch Republic could not and therefore suffered worst of all. Replacement was remarkably swift, but it must have meant a heavy capital expenditure, while when cattle numbers were low and supplies of organic manure consequently reduced, cereal yields were doubtless depressed. If so, the disadvantage over the cattle plagues was to the continent, and to Holland most of all. There was a definite value in farming on the scepter'd isle, in that the oppressed, war-weary peasants of mainland Europe would, with a given technology and size of holding, have higher production costs.

Second, the topographical underpinning of English farming systems gave rise to a special ability to innovate in one sector rather than in another. Agricultural systems in lowland Britain may essentially be divided into those on the free-draining soils of the chalk, limestone and more fertile sands, and those on the heavy, ill-drained clays. The available data show a much greater penetration of the 'new' crops and much more reclamation in the former group, and there are a few fragments of evidence to suggest that it was there that cereal output was rising. We may look on English agriculture as two machines. Producers operating the one (light land) were able to innovate by introducing the new forage crops, which proved so much more suitable for that environment. For instance, Houghton wrote in 1681, 'I have seen ground whose surface was deeply covered with white sand, as if it were poured from a sand-box, and there grew turnips . . . since *clover* and *santfoin* came in fashion, there is examples enough that areas that were not worth two shillings a year, are made worth thirty.'[1] Now that superior fodder crops were becoming widely available and were more worth growing to feed stock, the light land farmers found it possible to push cultivation onto former downs or rabbit warrens, using the sheepfold to put back more dung. They could raise their crop yields at lower unit costs. Their net receipts would rise, or at worst they might maintain their incomes in spite of spells of falling prices. Producers operating the other machine (heavy land) met serious technical obstacles in the

[1] Bradley, op. cit., p. 15.

way of introducing the new crops;[1] their output would be restrained; and when prices fell (partly because light land farmers were marketing more) their receipts would be squeezed.

Although these remarks about costs will remain conjectural until the laborious task of re-computing contemporary farm accounts has been faced, there is no doubt that a regional shift in arable farming did take place. It was not, of course, a simple or wholesale switch, for no simple dichotomy thrust on the continuum of farming systems can be adequate to explain the whole spectrum of responses from locality to locality within so varied a countryside as England's. Light land and heavy land systems do, however, seem to be the primary categories. They can reasonably be distinguished in terms of the available mix of factors of production and (at any given level of technology) their range of products. I believe this division to be more useful even than the overlapping but not precisely co-terminous distinction between enclosed and open-field areas. Whereas the evidence of a vigorous uptake of the 'new' crops comes mostly from the light land, the heavy land areas were slow to assimilate them.[2] Similarly, the evidence of poverty and distress among farmers stems mostly from the clay vales. These, where they had not been enclosed for grazing, were still largely farmed in open-field, and as John Evelyn reported of the East Midlands, in the open-field districts most of the rural houses were built of mud, 'and the people living as wretchedly as in the most impoverish'd parts of *France*, which the[y] much resemble being idle and sluttish.'[3] The question is, to what extent was the expansion of output and the income generated in the light land sector offset by the squeezing out of some part of production or income in the heavy land sector? No sudden, dramatic overturning of the distributions of agricultural production and profitability is to be anticipated, for responses to the market were likely to be dulled in the semi-developed agricultural economy of a pre-industrial society.[4] Nevertheless,

---

[1] M. H. R. Soper, 'Heavy Land Farming', *Agriculture*, LXVII (1960), pp. 174–8.

[2] See, e.g., G. H. Kenyon, 'Kirdford Inventories, 1611 to 1776, with Particular Reference to the Weald Clay Farming', *Sussex Archaeological Collections*, XCIII (1955), pp. 78–156, and C. W. Chalklin, 'The Rural Economy of a Kentish Wealden Parish, 1650–1750', *Agricultural History Review*, X (1962), pp. 29–45.

[3] De Beer, op. cit., III, p. 122 and n. 3.

[4] It is now known that considerable innovation did take place even within the communal husbandry sector, but progress there was blunted by the cumbersome decision-making apparatus of the open-field village, while with relatively poor flows of information in society as a whole, the diffusion of techniques was not rapid even in the 'severalty' sector.

despite the comparative torpor of the time, the light land and
heavy land sectors must have been in competition. The most
plausible reading is that there was a slow net expansion of agricultural output, attributable to the extension of mixed farming on
the light land at a time when exodus from the heavy land sector
was bound to be tardy. About 1680–85 Aubrey saw the whole
process as an exact balancing feat. Although his account of gains
in one sector and losses in the other is notably symmetrical, it may
not be too wide of the mark and it does provide a valuable insight
into the mechanics of adjustment:

> 'Great increase of sainfoine now, in most places fitt for itt;
> improvements of meadowes by watering; ploughing up of the
> King's forests and parkes &c. But as to all of these, as ten
> thousand pounds is gained in the hill barren countrey, so the
> vale does lose as much, which brings it to an equation.'[1]

V

Third, different situations obtained in England and on the
continent with regard to investment in land. The Restoration
settlement in England strengthened the landed magnates and
gave birth to rule by landed parliaments. An act of 1656 had
already abolished the Court of Wards, whereby the crown as
nominal owner of much land could exact feudal dues from the
operative landowners. The first business of the Commons in 1660,
once they had listened to the Declaration of Breda, was to confirm
the abolition.[2] The removal of these arbitrary dues fostered long-
term investment in estates. Parliament additionally threw open
the market place to practices which would maintain or raise the
value of land, practices which (because they might depopulate or
raise the price of grain) had been frowned on previously. An Act
of 1663 permitted regrating and engrossing (i.e. buying grain and
storing it for resale after the artificial scarcity had raised the
price), the aim being to stimulate the cultivation of 'wastes' by
rewarding 'the laying out of cost and labour.'[3] Acts were passed
which in the cause of improvement extinguished common rights
in the Great Level of the Fens and the Forest of Dean.[4]

[1] J. Britton (ed., *John Aubrey: The Natural History of Wiltshire* (Oxford 1847), p. 111.
[2] Hill, op. cit., p. 148.
[3] Ibid., p. 202.
[4] M. W. Beresford, 'Habitation versus Improvement', in F. J. Fisher (ed.), *Essays in the Economic and Social History of Tudor and Stuart England* (1961), p. 55 and n. 4.

Even during the Interregnum, moves to redistribute land in favour of small-scale, continental-style peasant farming were defeated, and parliament passed an Act to permit big undertakers to drain the Fens (despite popular protest) in the very month, May 1649, that the Levellers were cut down at Burford in Oxfordshire. Neither common rights nor copyhold tenure won absolute legal protection, which failure was thought by lawyer Blackstone in the eighteenth century to have been an immense boon to the ambitious property developer.[1] From the point of view of long-run agricultural development, given enthusiasm for agriculture among landowners, England had hit on a highly suitable distribution of land holding.

From the Restoration, or even the Interregnum, there does seem to have been an upsurge of 'improving' eagerness among the landed interest, fed to some extent by ideas picked up by Royalist exiles, recusants, merchants and mercenaries on the continent, especially in the initially more advanced Low Countries. Alert travellers originated from all over England. Even from the far north-west, Nicholas Blundell of Crosby in Lancashire visited Flanders, while at home he discussed fattening cattle & sheep in 'ye Beyond-Sea manner.'[2] Landowners were already eager in many cases to act as volunteer agencies for the promotion of agricultural development.

Yet the importance of the landowner lay not only in his cata-lytic role as innovator, significant as that was in the earliest stages of development, but also in his influence on investment levels in agriculture. The system in which a large share of the agricultural sector was operated on a landlord-tenant basis was peculiarly British. This offered two sources of capital, the landowner providing the capital-in-land (the farmland plus fixed equipment) and the tenant the working capital. Landowners customarily possessed extra-agricultural resources, such as mineral rights, urban rent-rolls, and the income from investments in government bonds, Bank of England stock and East India Company bonds. Their family fortunes had not infrequently been generated at court, in the law or in army posts. In 1726 one quarter of the active peerage held government or court offices.[3] Trade, notably

[1] Hill, op. cit., pp. 149–50.
[2] Margaret Blundell (ed.), *Blundell's Diary and Letter Book 1701–28* (1952) p. 132.
[3] G. E. Mingay, 'The Large Estate in Eighteenth-Century England', *Contributions: First International Conference of Economic History* (Paris, 1960), p. 373.

at this time colonial trade, was another important source of funds. Wealth amassed in the West Indian sugar plantations was especially prone to flow into landed estates in England; there are examples throughout the eighteenth century of returning 'West Indians' who busily set about improving their new estates. There are no estimates of the extent of this capital flow, but it was evidently large. George III and Pitt, while visiting Weymouth, met a 'Jamaican' with an equipage which the monarch thought too good for any but royalty. He burst out, 'sugar, sugar, eh?— all *that* sugar! How are the duties, eh, Pitt, how are the duties?'[1] Similarly, Irish officials were often absent from their posts, preferring reside and thus spend their salaries on English soil. Irish landowners, too, had a penchant for living on their English properties and disbursing Irish rents there. Calculations of 1728 put the flow of Irish wealth entering England at between £400,000 and £622,000 per annum. It was further argued that English merchants were enabled by higher rates of interest to retire earlier than Dutch merchants, to live off passive investments and to buy land.[2] Land offered these men social values, attested in the early eighteenth century by the willingness of purchasers of estates to forgo one per cent or one-and-a-half per cent interest on their money compared with the return they might have obtained outside agriculture, simply in order to enter the 'charmed circle' of English landed society. By these means, cheap capital was siphoned into agriculture, freeing the farm operator's resources for day-to-day uses. Admittedly, the case studies on which this interpretation is based are few, and the prospects of adding much to our slender stock of reconstructed estate accounts are poor given the resources now available to students, but we may note that one contemporary observer, Macpherson, wrote more generally in 1729 of great sums lately spent on enclosing and improving land.[3] Whatever the broader effects of this diversion of capital from the rest of the economy, as well as the diversion of entrepreneurial talent at an early age which contemporaries complained about, the result could not be but to stimulate the agricultural sector.

---

[1] L. J. Ragatz, *The Fall of the Planter Class in the British Caribbean, 1763–1833* (New York, 1963), p. 50; R. B. Sheridan, 'The Wealth of Jamaica in the Eighteenth Century', *Econ. Hist. Rev.* 2nd ser. XVIII (1965), especially pp. 304–9.

[2] R. B. Westerfield, *Middlemen in English Business 1660–1760* (Yale, 1915), pp. 372–3, 402–3.

[3] *Annals of Commerce*, III, p. 147, quoted by Toynbee, op. cit., p. 45.

These dual sources of capital for English agriculture lifted it out of the rut of capital-scarcity and indebtedness so widespread in European peasant farming. Whereas in some continental countries restrictions were placed on the sale of land to men not of noble birth, in England there was no such barrier. Land was secure; the device of the strict settlement prevented fresh generations from breaking-up the family estate; the emergence of the long-term mortgage about the middle of the seventeenth century (together with a fall in the rate of interest, usually 10 per cent to landowners before 1625, from 1680 seldom topping 5 per cent)[1] made borrowing for land improvement much easier. In England the public sale of honours had ended, but since social status attached to land-owning men who could no longer buy peerages invested in their estates.[2] On the continent, in contrast, social privileges were distinct from the ownership of land: a seignorial title, as, for example, Slicher van Bath (of Bath in Zealand) does not necessarily imply the ownership of land at Bath. In Holland after about 1650 moneyed men formed a strictly urban patriciate, the *regentiepatriciaat*, some with seignorial titles but without land, most devoting the profits of their public offices (which in England would have been inevitably a step on the road to a dignified country park) to town houses and fine pictures, not the laying of field to field and the rearing of fat beasts. Englishmen were content with *pieds à terre* in town. Whereas on the continent social structures efficiently diverted capital from the land, in England they constantly pumped it in that direction. To take another continental example, in France the grandees were absentees, rentiers who were obliged to reside at court but who owned seigneuries and received huge incomes from exercising feudal rights and exacting tolls. They found this amply profitable with less outlay and trouble than engaging in agricultural improvement. A fashion for hobby farming and the physiocratic desire to replace peasant 'subsistence' farming with farming by proprietors for a saleable surplus, came in the following period. The peasants who owned their own land necessarily had to find both fixed and working capital, and were deprived of a cushion against depression. Furthermore, in the reign of Louis XIV the nobility tried

---

[1] H. J. Habakkuk, 'The English Land Market in the Eighteenth Century', in J. S. Bromley and E. H. Kossman (eds.), *Britain and the Netherlands* (London, 1960), p. 160.
[2] Hill, op. cit., p. 204.

to bid up its exclusiveness by blocking the entry into its ranks of those who had made money in trade, thus robbing French agriculture of the regular injections of merchant capital which were so conspicuous a feature in England.

Although on English tenant farms the level of rent was nominally fixed, landowners regularly remitted or 'allowed' some proportion of the payment due, or let arrears mount up, in years of falling prices. The system was apparently devised to maximize estate revenue over the long-run, and the existence on paper of agreed rents was seldom permitted to banish temporarily embarrassed tenants from agriculture. Whereas tenants tended to depend on year-to-year farm income, landowners often possessed not only greater staying power through their extra-agricultural resources, but dynastic ambitions; they planned to maximize returns over some generations, and to do so they were prepared to forgo some part of current rent in order to preserve the fabric of their tenantry. In addition, landowners might step into the breach and make additional fixed investments designed to expand the productive capacity of the farm, and even stray over into providing some working capital, like grass seeds. The larger landowners, who were gaining relative to the lesser gentry at this period, were most active in this way.

Why should landowners have been willing to invest resources in agriculture at such a time? Did the social prestige of land not attach simply to the broad acres rather than to the condition of farming on them? Part of the answer is that the value system of English landed society did take account of the technical excellence of agriculture. The fever of improvement may not have burned as it was to at the end of the eighteenth century, but it was already heating the brow in many cases. Besides the ingredient of sheer enthusiasm for hobby farming, it has been said that 'the pressure of the rising costs of high living on the landowners introduces a uniquely English factor into rural improvement.'[1] A number of landowners was said to have entered deeply into debt in order to support an elegant style of life (London and provincial seasons, horse-racing and the associated wagering, Grand Tours and above all mansion building). These individuals, or some of them, apparently attempted to recoup by enlarging their rent rolls, by equipping their tenants to increase output at lower unit costs.

[1] Wilson, op. cit., p. 262.

Some enclosures had been put under way by Royalist families because they were hard-pressed as early as the Interregnum.[1] But while it is acceptable that socio-dynastic ambition might have induced many landowners to take a lower return than they might have reaped in commerce or industry, can we really think that indebted men, who clearly must place the highest premium on rapid returns, would plunge deep into improving their estates unless there was a good chance of profit in agriculture? The conclusion must surely be that apart from short-term difficulties English agriculture, even grain production, was satisfactorily profitable during the 1650–1750 period.

VI

The potency of a fourth special feature of English agriculture, the Corn Bounties, is less obvious. Certainly, such a subsidy was without foreign parallel, just as it was contrary to the English precedent of concern for the consumer's rather than the producer's interest, but its long-run consequences cannot be dogmatically stated. In the short run the bounties represented a gain for the growers of cereals. The landowner-dominated Restoration parliaments had offered a bounty on grain exports by an Act of 1673, and the law was amended still further in agriculture's favour in succeeding spells of very low prices. There are surviving letters of 1675 or '76 suggesting that the bounty straightaway induced merchants to step up their purchases of grain for export, raising the price to the farmer.[2] This presumably stimulated production, and may conceivably have done so in bursts after later amendments of the law. If so, the enlarged supply would have tended to reduce the price in the long run. Any assessment of whether farmers as a body would then have earned more (or less) by selling an increased output at a slightly lower unit price depends on sheer guesswork about the elasticities of demand for grain.[3] If demand

[1] H. J. Habakkuk, 'Landowners and the Civil War', *Econ. Hist. Rev.* 2nd ser. XVIII (1965), p. 138 and n. 3.

[2] Letters quoted by E. Lipson, *The Economic History of England* (London, 1934), II, p. 453.

[3] A highly relevant dispute between Fay and Lipson over the effects of the bounties may be approached through T. S. Ashton's review of C. R. Fay, *The Corn Laws and Social England*, in *Econ. J.* XLIII (1933), p. 478. It has been usual to suggest that the demand for wheat was inelastic, but very recently Mr Flinn has pointed to the eighteenth-century substitution of wheat for coarser grains as perhaps reflecting quite high elasticities. ('Agricultural Productivity and Economic Growth in England, 1700–1760: A Comment', *Journ. Econ. Hist.* XXVI (1966), p. 97). It is also possible that western European demand elasticities for English cereals were high.

were inelastic and the effect of the bounties to depress total farm income, English landed interests had devised a short-run carrot with a propensity for turning into a long-run stick. In that case, we have to attribute the comparative buoyancy of English agriculture and its ability to develop technically and institutionally at this time, as has been suggested above, to the advantages of an island site, to the competitive internal adjustments of English farming systems, and to the mobilization of an unusual flow of capital for agricultural use. If, on the other hand, demand elasticities were high, the bounties may have tended to assist these other forces in raising total farm income despite poor product prices. And if that were so, it would mean that income drawn largely from taxes on land in general was in England being redistributed in favour of the arable sector, which would help in explaining the atypical level of activity in English cereal growing at this period.

VII

The new husbandry systems which evolved in England were mixed, that is they integrated the production of cereals and livestock on the same land, whereas on the continent there appears to have been a much more sweeping transfer of land from cereal-growing into pastoral farming, or in some cases even out of production altogether. In England the separation of arable and grass had already been blurred during the early modern period, by the development of alternate husbandry, which by resting land from cereal production under grass instead of leaving it fallow made some increase in output possible. Yet, without falling into the trap of assigning all significant changes in so slow-moving a group of industries to the semi-arbitrary period 1650–1750, the widespread adoption of forage crops (and irrigated pasture) at this time enormously racked up agriculture's productive capacity. The growth of mixed farming *via* the insertion of fodder crops into the English arable fields sparked off what may be thought of as a virtually self-propelling spiral. Adam Smith made a revealing analysis of the interactions of crop and animal production within mixed farming, and their role in the whole process of economic development in seventeenth- and eighteenth-century Britain. He argued that once set in motion by a rise in livestock prices (and the period saw what was more relevant, a rise in these prices relative to cereals) sufficient to induce the improvement of land simply to feed animals, this improvement would be communicated to the whole of agriculture. The process would be inexorable, though slow: 'the increase of stock and the improvement of land are two events which must go hand in hand, and of which the one can no-where much out-run the other.'[1]

Recently a similar kind of thesis, which we may perhaps designate a 'technical linkages' theory, has been elaborated in more precise historical detail in a study of open-field farming in Oxfordshire.[2] This revealed the process whereby the growing of more forage crops had a feedback effect on subsequent yields of cereals through the increased supply of better quality dung. Subsequent fodder crops, too, reaped this benefit, so that as long as prevailing livestock prices made a minimum return possible the 'new' crops were virtually able to create their own demand for store animals to feed them off. An eighteenth-century writer conceived the advantages in this way: 'the most profitable soil to inclose is a sandy or light loam, where the cultivation of turnips, clover and the artificial grasses can be effected with certain success . . . On such soil abundance of food for stock is produced, which generally furnishes a great quantity of rich manure for the arable land, so that the business of farming and grazing together are much more advantageously pursued than either can be to any great extent without the other.'[3] Thus there were within mixed farming systems peculiar external economies for cereal growing arising from the production of livestock on the same land. Given these fruitful linkages we may expect that output would rise except as offset by the withdrawal of inferior clay land from crop production, and that output would be more balanced in composition than on the average holding in western Europe, where many farmers were switching right out of cereals. It would be interesting if we could be sure that the ratios of livestock: cereal prices had risen further in mainland European countries than in England.

The ultimate advantages of mixed farming were considerable.

[1] Edwin Cannan (ed.), *Adam Smith: The Wealth of Nations* (New York, 1937; first edition, 1776), Book I, Chapter XI, pp. 219–28.
[2] M. A. Havinden, 'Agricultural Progress in Open-field Oxfordshire', *Agric. Hist. Rev.* IX (1961), pp. 73–83.
[3] T. Stone, *Suggestions for Rendering the Inclosure of Common Fields and Waste Lands a Source of Population and Riches* (1787), pp. 26–7.

The system was an 'expanding circle' which when stepped up would yield all-round increments. The potential productivity of England's developing agriculture is obvious, but it may be as well to anticipate the question as to why, if technical advance before 1750 was as marked as this essay has contended, food prices rose thereafter and the third quarter of the century was so punctuated by food riots. The answer seems to be that cereal production, much of which had still not shifted onto the more freely-draining soils, was depressed by an abnormal number of wet seasons. Without such changes as there had been, this period would surely have been much more damaging than it turned out. Writing in 1774 Gilbert White observed that the 'corn vales' had been drowned for ten or eleven seasons past, since 'land-springs have never obtained more since the memory of man than during that period; nor has there been known a greater scarcity of all sorts of grain, considering the great improvements of modern husbandry. Such a run of wet seasons a century or two ago would, I am persuaded, have occasioned a famine.'[1] Despite poor harvests on the supply side and swelling population on the demand side, by the late 1770s English agriculture had again overfilled its markets and brought prices down. The whole agricultural structure was still by later standards cumbersome and slow to react, but the changes of the 1650–1750 period had made it much more viable than ever before. An advanced form of mixed farming had emerged on light lands which in the mid-seventeenth century had been lying as sheep pasture since the High Middle Ages. Had this productive asset been the sole reward for England's distinctive response to the low price level of that hundred years, it would have been well worth acquiring.

The agricultural innovations of this period may, further, have been of great consequence in reshaping the distributions of economic activity within England. This possibility will deserve investigation. Mixed farming developed fastest on the lighter soils of the southern half of England, including the dry eastern counties which are naturally the least suited to growing grass and other feed crops. East Anglia, ironically enough, was the most difficult district in which to ensure that a crop of turnips would 'take'. Before this period the north and west (where in the eternal damp grass grows strongly) had been much more vigorously

[1] *The Natural History of Selborne* (London, 1949 edn.), pp. 168–9.

competitive in livestock production. Thereafter, although the north remained the supplier of store stock, the south was vastly better able to feed and fatten animals, and therefore to reap the return of their manure. The inducement to expand farm production in the south was doubtless greater because demand was initially higher there. The agricultural capacity of the south, relative to the north, must have taken a big leap forward. Quite understandably, therefore, the northern graziers wished 'to obtain a law to suppress the Improvements in the Southern Parts.'[1] The consequences of their failure may have been enormous. Could it be that the rise of industry in the north, and its withering in the south, was due in a significant measure to a definite shift in comparative advantage caused by regionally disparate agricultural innovation? Certainly the mechanism whereby southern farm profits came to be transmitted northwards would assume critical importance, since the effect of the innovations in farming may have been to make a decisive separation between the area of strongest demand for industrial capital and the zone where the highest level of profit was generated in agriculture.

In addition to likely regional shifts, another issue which is raised is the implication of the agricultural changes for the scale and timing of expansion in the industrial sector. This of course is the main relevance of the agricultural aspect of economic growth in the eighteenth century. Why did cheaper food release too few resources to produce any marked upturn in the physical output of industry? It may be that the net release of real income through cheaper bread was rather slight—much depends on the interpretation of a few series of institutional purchase prices of wheat since so far little effort has been made to extract and publish better figures. Possibly much of the potential rise in income was cancelled out by depressive tendencies in the heavy land sector. All these questions merit explicit examination in the course of local studies. Beyond this, we have perhaps to fall back on the argument that early eighteenth century labour had a high leisure preference and a backward-sloping supply curve of effort. Petty, whose father was a clothier at Romsey in Hampshire, made it evident that this interpretation was at least dear to contemporaries: 'It was observed by clothiers and others who employ great numbers of poor people, that when corn is extremely plentiful that

[1] See footnote 2 on page 60.

the labour of the poor is proportionately dear and scarce to be had at all, so licentious are they who labour only to eat, or rather to drink.'[1] If such tastes were at all general, the mass market for industrial goods would be very weak. Yet England had become a country with high expectations of welfare. English workmen went shod in leather, not wooden clogs; they ate well of wheaten bread, not rye. These habits may have been auspicious for the emergence of an industrial economy. Undisciplined in the past, the chances were that when the cost-of-living rose in the second half of the eighteenth century Englishmen would work harder in order to preserve as much as possible of this level and pattern of consumption. Whatever the precise explanation of the deferred pay-off of agricultural change, there can, however, be no doubt that the years 1650–1750 saw a marked expansion of the capacity of English agriculture to produce.

In contrast, England's main rival in industry and international trade, the Netherlands, saw her once equally mature agriculture weakened; her reliance on imported grain was doubtless a liability in the dear times later in the eighteenth century,[2] when the Dutch again attempted to expand their own cereal farming. Charles Wilson has argued that high food costs and high taxes (for defence) gave rise to high labour costs, and that these were the main cause of the inability of the Dutch to compete industrially and of the emergence of swarms of poor in the Netherlands in the eighteenth century.[3] Thus, by the standards of all the grossly under-developed world in which they lived, Englishmen at this period were already well-to-do and capable of greatly expanding

---

[1] Lord Edmond Fitzmaurice, *The Life of Sir William Petty 1623–1687* (London, 1895), p. 220.

[2] Quite apart from a deteriorating position as import prices rose, the Dutch might be virtually cut off from external supplies in a world of warring nation states. For instance, in the winter of 1771–72, 'the Dutch were in the greatest distress for want of corn and cattle, having received little or no supply from Poland, the usual granary of the north (which was now ravaged and desolated by the inroads of the neighbouring powers) or from any other of the corn or pasture countries; whereupon the small quantity of provisions they possessed, or obtained, rose to a most enormous price. Such, notwithstanding the opinion of a very great political economist, must sometimes be the consequence of a nation depending entirely upon others for the first of necessaries, even though there should be the most unbounded freedom of commerce in their ports.' David MacPherson, *Annals of Commerce* (London, 1805), III, p. 519.

[3] Charles Wilson, 'Taxation and the Decline of Empire', *Bijdragen en Mededelingen van het Historisch Genootschap, Utrecht*, LXXVII (1963), pp. 10–26.

their already well-developed agriculture. As Samuel Sorbiere said of them in his *Voyage to England*:[1]

'I am very ready to excuse the roughness of a people who live in so fine a country, who cultivate a soil that yields them plenty of all necessaries for human life, who besides all these conveniences find themselves surrounded by the sea, which is a fence to secure them from other nations . . . 'Tis a natural enough thing for people who have so good a share, to despise all the rest of mankind.'

[1] Of 1663. Quoted as a heading in Arthur Koestler (ed.), *Suicide of a Nation?* (New York, 1964).

4

N. VON TUNZELMANN

Technological Diffusion during the Industrial Revolution: The Case of the Cornish Pumping Engine

I

As most attention has been centred on Lancashire, the West Riding of Yorkshire, and the Midlands, it frequently comes as a surprise to re-discover that one of the most technologically-advanced machines of the early nineteenth century was developed in the far South-west, in Cornwall. A roll-call of inventors by birth immediately suggests the role of the South-west in steam engines: from the Devonians Savery and Newcomen at the turn of the eighteenth century, through Jonathan Hornblower to Richard Trevithick and Arthur Woolf in the early nineteenth century. Of the British inventors and engineers of first rank directly associated with improving the steam engine, up to say 1850, perhaps only Smeaton and Watt are excluded from this list. Moreover, both Smeaton and Watt were to have great impact upon Cornish mining; and both men, Watt especially, were profoundly influenced in the nature of their improvements by the demands of the Cornish miners.

Trevithick erected what is generally regarded as the first Cornish pumping engine at the Wheal Prosper mine in 1812; a high-pressure condensing engine. The amalgamation of high-pressure steam with its subsequent condensation was principally the work of Arthur Woolf, originally using a compound (i.e. two-cylinder) engine. Engines of this type, with or without compounding, found their way to water-works in many parts of England before 1850.[1] They proved popular overseas, notably in

---

[1] Thomas Wicksteed, *Further Elucidations of the Useful Effects of Cornish Pumping Engines*, (London, 1859), recounts the performance of two Cornish engines at the Old Ford Water-works. The *Civil Engineer and Architect's Journal*, vol. II, 1839, records a Cornish-built engine being installed at Carlisle.

France, where theorists repeatedly advocated their use in the interests of greatest fuel economy.[1] From an engineer's point of view, the technical sophistication of an engine could be inferred from the efficiency with which it transformed energy so as to produce useful work. By the 1820s and 1830s there can be little doubt that the best Cornish engine produced the greatest amount of useful effect from a given quantity of coals consumed of any engine then in existence.

In the last few years several major studies of the Cornish engine, especially those of D. B. Barton and T. R. Harris, have dispelled much of the recent ignorance.[2] These books, however, are predominantly industrial archaeologies. Few good studies of nineteenth-century Cornish economic history have appeared since W. J. Rowe's *Cornwall in the Age of the Industrial Revolution*. But Rowe is largely concerned with economic fluctuations in the Cornish mining industry as a whole, and therefore his attention is directed towards copper and tin rather than to engines as such. The present article hopefully aims to peer into the half-light by trying to elucidate some of the economic aspects of technological progress. Even though the results are relatively simple, nevertheless they have few parallels in the economic history of this period.

In the present instance such results are possible because detailed reports were issued monthly from August, 1811, by the Lean family. For each engine investigated every month (at the rate of one guinea a visit), they published its performance (load lifted, length of stroke, number of strokes per minute, etc.) as well as general remarks on the pumps, state of the boilers, cylinder size, and so on.[3] One column of the reports gave 'lbs. raised one foot high per bushel of coals consumed', or as it was called by contemporary Cornish engineers, the 'duty' of the engine. It is to be noted that, unlike horse-power, duty measures the thermodynamic efficiency of an engine, since the divisor is total fuel consumption in the relevant month. It is possible to derive horse-

---

[1] See, e.g., Baron Dupin, *Rapport fait à l'Institut de France* . . . (Académie Royale des Sciences), (Paris, 1823); and P. Grouvelle et A. Jaunez, *Guide du Chauffeur et du Propriétaire de Machines à Vapeur* (4th ed.) (Paris, 1858/9).

[2] D. B. Barton, *The Cornish Beam Engine* (Truro, 1965); T. R. Harris, *Arthur Woolf: the Cornish Engineer, 1766–1837* (Truro, 1966).

[3] A nearly complete set of the *Engine Reporter* is now held at the Redruth Public Library. I wish to thank the librarians and staff of that library; the Royal Institution of Cornwall Museum, Truro; the Cornwall County Record Office, Truro; the Plymouth City Library; and the National Reference Library of Science and Invention (Holborn Division), London; for their special exertions on my behalf.

power from the duty figures with knowledge of the coal consumption and of the precise time period involved for that consumption (and both of these are supplied in the Reports).[1] However, duty reflects practical performance to a greater degree; it allows for frictions generated through the application of the power source to particular conditions of pitwork and pumping equipment. Thus the realised horse-power which might be derived in this way would be less than 'actual horse-power'. More importantly, duty is a measure of the productivity of the largest variable input into steam engines, so that it can be more directly put to use to construct an index of diffusion of a new technology. Horse-power can be increased over a very wide range by building larger and larger engines embodying exactly the same engineering know-how. In Diagram I, the duty and horse-power of Taylor's 70-inch engine at the Consolidated Mines are charted for 1827–33. After 1829, although the technical improvements of the kind described below are installed, horse-power continues to rise quite rapidly, presumably through more intensive driving. Duty, on the other hand, stays virtually constant.[2]

'Duty', then, indicates the amount of water pumped out (output) per unit of coal input. There is every indication of a qualitative kind that the goal of Cornish engineers (the criterion of their efficiency) was to maximize the duty of the engines they were entrusted with. In some cases the managers paid their engineers 'million money'[3] as a bonus for raising duty. The very publication of Lean's 'Engine Reporter' was both a symptom of and a stimulus to the competitive spirit prevailing between rival engineers over duty. Accordingly, a body of data is available on precisely the kind of improvement that these engineers most desired to make.

How reliable are these reports? In them, duty was calculated from four observations:

(i). The total weight of water in the pumps. The most serious criticism contemporaries levelled at the duty figures was that they

---

[1] To derive horse-power from duty, multiply duty by the monthly consumption of coals then divide by 33,000 times the number of minutes actually worked during the month.

[2] These figures for duty and horse-power are taken from J. Farey, *Treatise on the Steam Engine*, vol II, n.d. This second volume of Farey's superb Treatise was never published but a copy in typescript survives with MS. corrections in the N.R.L.S.I., Chancery Lane. The whole of this second volume is devoted to the Cornish engine.

[3] The reason for such a term will become obvious below.

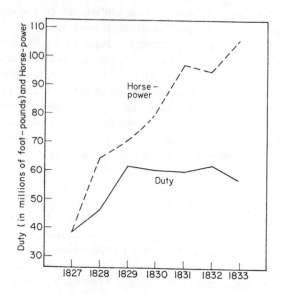

DIAGRAM I. Annual averages of duty and horse-power
for Taylor's engine, Consolidated Mines, 1827–33.

were based not on the actual weight of water pumped out, but on
the amount that ought to have been pumped out at each stroke.
Discrepancies between one and the other would arise if the pumps
were drawing air along with the water, when the engine was said
to be 'in fork'. This occurred where the mine was kept well
drained such that the water was being drawn from the bottom of
the mine. A season of low rainfall could therefore see higher
duties being registered than the same engines would have been
capable of had the weather been very wet.[1] It is probably super-
fluous to observe that in Cornwall a long run of very dry seasons
was highly unlikely.

In calculating duty, the weight of water was taken as the total
contents of the pumps multiplied by a given constant, the weight
of a cubic foot of fresh water. Minerals in suspension in the water
could corrode the pumps over time, thereby inducing leakages.

[1] Farey thought this the reason why the Watt engine at Stray Park shaft, commonly
regarded as the best Watt engine in Cornwall before the native Cornish improvements,
attained duties over 30 millions in 1814 and early 1815. The use of high-quality fuel is a
much more probable explanation, though seasonal climatic irregularities may have contributed.

On this score, the actual quantity of water pumped out may have fallen short of the theoretical delivery. On the other hand, most mines pumped water that was far from being fresh spring water and normally weighed a good deal more than the assumed constant.

(ii). The length of stroke in the pumps—this was equal to the length of piston stroke in the cylinder multiplied by the proportion of the great beam beyond its pivot ('outdoors'). The length of the indoor stroke could be altered by adjusting the tappets, etc., but careful account of any alterations seems to have been kept. However, the quoted length of stroke was the full distance the piston could travel before hitting the cylinder bottom; in practice it would be stopped a few inches short to prevent accidents from the piston going too far. Farey reckoned the deficiency of actual length compared with reported length to be on an average $1/25$ in 1816.[1] This deficiency was probably ameliorated over time, from better management of the engines particularly with the use of indicators, and from increases in the length of cylinder of many engines later in the period. To this extent, the rate of technical progress would be understated.

(iii). The number of strokes made by the engine in the whole month. This figure registered on a special counter, kept locked so that only the reporters had access to it. The counter was not infallible—in particular, it could not take account of occasional shortening of the piston stroke. A four months' test of a counter on a large engine at the United Mines in 1839 showed that on the average the counter read about $2\frac{1}{2}$ per cent too high.[2]

(iv). Coal consumption. The total number of bushels of coal consumed in the 'month' (which could be anything from three to five weeks) between the visits of the reporters divides into the product of (i), (ii), and (iii), to give the monthly duty. Pole in 1844 stated that the coal was measured every day by the employee as he barrowed in the requisite quantity.[3] But by the early 1850s in many cases the coal figures were taken from invoices, with deductions for the coal remaining in stock little more than guesses of the size of the heap. Sometimes, according to Barton, the monthly 'guesstimates' fell well short of annual purchases, taken

[1] Farey, op. cit., p. 178.
[2] N. Trestrail, 'The Duty of Cornish Pumping Engines, Past and Present', *Journal of the South Staffordshire Institution of Mining Engineers, 1896*.
[3] W. Pole, *A Treatise on the Cornish Pumping Engine* (London, 1844), p. 147.

from the invoices.[1] For the present, this refers to the end of our period, when overstatement is a minor concern.

Before the 1850s a more common criticism was that the bushel was a measure of volume rather than weight. In theory, a bushel of coal weighed 84 lbs, but the good Welsh coal used in Cornwall had a high density and in practice the Cornish bushel was often put at 94 lbs.—officially so by the 1830s. In December, 1831, Lean weighed a bushel of coal at 31 mines; the results from 15 mines show variations from 88 to 97 lbs.[2] The wetness of the coal also affected the weight of a bushel. Thus Wicksteed went to great trouble to overcome this source of variation by insisting on actually weighing all the coal used in his tests at the Old Ford Water-works, London.[3] From the mid-1850s the Leans themselves used cwts. rather than bushels as deflators to derive duty. William Pole maintained that a volume measure was preferable to a weight to evaluate the duty since in his opinion it provided a more consistent index of actual energy input.[4] More significantly, in studying the economic aspects of changes in average duty, it is relevant that until the end of 1836 coal in Cornwall was purchased by the bushel (or wey of 64 bushels); i.e. the bushel and not the cwt., was what should rationally have entered managerial considerations.

Virtually every conceivable source of error of measurement has now been dealt with, and it remains to ask after their effects on the conclusions of this paper. The answer must be very little. Factors such as the steam space left in the cylinder at the end of each stroke were common to all engines (indeed the proportion left in Boulton and Watt engines was larger than in the Cornish), so that comparisons with other types of engine are hardly invalidated. But the major worry is short-term biases that may creep into calculations of rates of technological diffusion, etc. Partly for this reason, statistical methods are developed in later parts of this paper that attempt to annul the effects of random short-run discrepancies.

The difficulty in the present instance is less errors of measurement than estimating how representative the sample is. Intuitively one might expect only the better engines to be submitted for reporting. Certainly the miscellaneous winding and stamping

---

[1] Barton, op. cit., pp. 59–60.
[2] Figures quoted in Farey, op. cit.
[3] T. Wicksteed, *An Experimental Inquiry concerning Cornish and Boulton and Watt Pumping Engines* . . . (London, 1841).
[4] Pole, op. cit., p. 155.

engines found at many mines, and some of the smaller pumping engines as well, would barely be worth the monthly fee as their aggregate coal consumption (and hence opportunity for absolute fuel economy) was so low. The neglect of these smaller engines limits discussion of e.g. the diffusion of best-practice techniques to the more powerful pumping engines, those for which economy of fuel was important in determining the overall profitability of the mine.

In 1838, W. J. Henwood took a careful census of mine engines in the South-west.[1] Excluding Devon (where only four engines were listed) Henwood noted 150 pumping engines. Of these 150 no less than seventy appeared in Lean's *Engine Reporter* for the years 1837–8 and at least a further twenty were reported in other years, so that 60 per cent of the counted engines appear at some stage in our figures. After the late 1830s the number of engines reported drops off rapidly, while the total number of Cornish engines seems to have continued to increase. For the bulk of this study, then, the analysis is taken only as far as the late 1830s. Relating to size of engine, 36 per cent of engines recorded by Henwood with cylinder diameter of less than 40 inches appeared at some time in the *Reporter*, while 72 per cent of those of 40 inches or more appeared.

Shreds of comparable evidence on the duty of engines in Cornwall tend to confirm the view that Lean's *Reporter* gave exaggerated attention to the more powerful engines. From 1834, one William Tonkin issued reports on some of the engines the Leans did not cover. None of Tonkin's reports seem to have survived, but Farey extracted and summarized some of their content.[2] In one table, Farey calculated annual averages of duty for every engine in both the Lean and Tonkin reports combined. These averages are shown in Table I, for 1832–39, together with equivalent averages based solely on Lean taken from Lemon and other sources.[3] It will be noted that different methods of averaging give slightly different average duty figures even in 1832–3 before Tonkin began. The estimate of the number of engines surveyed by Tonkin is also approximate.

[1] William Jory Henwood, *The Metalliferous Deposits of Cornwall and Devon* (Penzance and London, 1843).
[2] Farey, op. cit., especially p. 252.
[3] Sir Charles Lemon, 'The Statistics of the Copper Mines of Cornwall', *J. Stat. Soc.*, vol. I, June 1838.

Table I

ANNUAL AVERAGES OF DUTY RECORDED BY THE REPORTED ENGINES IN
CORNWALL, 1832–39

(in millions of foot-pounds per bushel of coal)

	1832	1833	1834	1835	1836	1837	1838	1839
1. From Farey	44·5	46·12	46·64	46·49	46·60	46·50	46·82	46·85
2. From other sources	45·04	46·63	47·84	48·21	46·65	47·09	48·7	52·8
3. No. of engines in Tonkin's reports	—	—	5	16	11	13	11	23

Farey's series remains practically constant after 1833; the other based on Lean alone rises perceptibly after 1836. Another of Farey's tables, listing all engines reported by Lean and Tonkin in 1835 according to cylinder size, enables further comparison: Lean reports 26 engines with cylinder diameters less than 60 inches and 29 of 60 inches and above; Tonkin 10 and 9 respectively.[1]

The Leans themselves commented upon the 'scale effects' of larger engines attaining higher duties.[2] In Table II a simplified version of one of the tables in their *Historical Statement* is presented, showing average annual duty by diameter of cylinder (i.e. roughly by 'nominal horse-power' in James Watt's sense) at seven-year intervals, 1814 to 1835:

Table II

AVERAGE ANNUAL DUTY, BY ENGINE SIZE
(in millions)

Cylinder size	1814	1821	1828	1835
Under 30 inches	14·33	19·91	26·47	34·22
30–40 ,,	18·46	23·04	26·43	38·12
40–50 ,,	19·86	28·40	33·37	45·04
50–60 ,,	20·08	29·10	34·76	48·75
60–70 ,,	23·36	28·45	41·37	52·17
70–80 ,,	31·21	38·01	54·08	64·39
80–90 ,,	27·44	33·41	47·88	55·12

With minor exceptions, the table indicates economies being obtained up to 80-inch engines, then diseconomies setting in for the largest class of engines.

[1] The hypothesis that the proportion of large and small engines in the two sets of reports could have come from populations with different distributions was rejected at the 95 per cent level of confidence in a 2 × 2 contingency table.

[2] T. and J. Lean, *Historical Statement of the Improvements made in the Duty Performed by the Steam Engines in Cornwall* . . . (London and Camborne, 1839).

The life history of a typical engine can be sketched in briefly. In the first few months of operation its duty normally rose. The most important reasons for this include: (i) the time required to find any leaks in the pumping equipment and to stop them; (ii) experience had to be gained in managing the fires and dampers optimally; (iii) the size of fire grates and number of boilers actually used could be varied; (iv) the most suitable way to regulate feed water entering the boilers had to be discovered; (v) in this period of rather primitive lubricants, allowing any irregularities in rubbing surfaces to wear themselves smooth; (vi) finding the strength at which the steam was best supplied to the cylinder, and the length to which its expansion could best be carried. To summarize, there was an initial period of learning about every engine, for each had its individual quirks. Thus some of the above relate to deficiencies in the construction of the engine itself. Others have reference to the particular context to which the engine is applied, e.g. in the long run, the extent to which expansion was carried depended on the weight of pit-work and balances to be lifted; because if these were too light, very high expansion would involve large fluctuations during each stroke in the rate at which power was transmitted, subjecting the machinery to great strain. (This was one reason why the more powerful engines tended to achieve higher duties.)

Gains in duty through the learning process increased at a diminishing rate and eventually were outweighed by physical deterioration. Cornish engines were run 24 hours a day, so that this decline could be quite rapid, and overhauls soon called for. Any stoppage in the pumping action usually meant not just a zero advance but positive retrogression, with the mine going out of fork and filling up with water. Important sources of physical decline were (i) the engines, pumps and pit-work simply wearing out; (ii) leakages from the boilers into the fires becoming considerable; (iii) increased loads imposed on the engine by new pumps as the mine deepened, especially if the new shafts were not vertical but inclined, as often occurred in the 1840s and subsequently; (iv) even without increased loads, the plates of the boilers wore thin and the pressure of the steam had to be reduced for safe operation.

The Cornish engine departed from traditional British steam-engine practice most significantly in its use of high-pressure steam and expansion. Unlike most high-pressure American engines of the time, however, the Cornish engine retained the principle of condensing the steam, in this case after expansion had reduced its pressure to near atmospheric levels. Strictly speaking the engine was what the French referred to as a 'machine à moyenne pression': from 1850 Lean published the mean pressures of steam in the boilers of each engine reported, and in that year the highest pressure was 50 lb. per square inch (for one engine only), 42 lb. p.s.i. being the next highest, and the arithmetic mean 34½ lb. The principal reason for not using higher pressures was the desire to avoid the resulting stresses in the situation of round-the-clock work mentioned above. Still, such pressures were considerably higher than for most other stationary steam engines in Britain before 1850.

Boulton and Watt had made use of expansion of the steam inside the cylinder before condensation as early as 1785 in some of their engines in Cornwall. But so long as the steam from the boiler was kept at or little above atmospheric pressure, expansion could not be taken very far. Jonathan Hornblower had earlier attempted to develop the use of expansion by constructing the first compound engine, but the advantages of the Hornblower engines vis-à-vis the Watt type were never clearly demonstrated, since low-pressure steam continued to be used.[1] Trevithick was the first Englishman to adopt high-pressure steam. In terms of economic significance, however, Arthur Woolf was much greater a figure in their native Cornwall. Woolf's engines combined Trevithick's use of high-pressure steam with Hornblower's of compounding in two cylinders. Subsequently the expansion and condensation phases were both carried out in a single cylinder, although a number of engines were compounding much later in our period, presaging the multiple compounding that was to characterize the most efficent steam engines of the latter nineteenth century.

In the late 1820s, further advance took the forms of much more extensive and careful use of steam jacketing and the clothing of all steam pipes, etc. By these and similar means the steam was in effect being superheated, twenty years and more before the theory underlying superheating was spelled out. Surface condensation

---

[1] Rhys Jenkins, 'Jonathan Hornblower and the Compound Engine', *Transactions of the Newcomen Society*, vol. XI, 1931.

along the lines used generally after 1850 was also experimented with, e.g. by Trevithick.[1]

To trace the growth in duty that these technical improvements induced, the March figure of duty performed has been taken for every reported engine for every year from 1812 to 1852. March was selected so as to avoid on the one hand the summer season when mines would be relatively dry and since loads would be light the duty figures be artificially high; and on the other winter, when the converse applied. If March figures were unavailable, e.g. because the boilers were being repaired or the counter was idle, April or sometimes February duty was used, even October in desperation. Not counting entries in the *Engine Reporter* for which no duty was actually given (for example, coal consumption was sometimes missing), this procedure gave a sample of 16 in 1812, rising quickly to 37 in 1816 then more gradually to 60 in 1828 and unevenly to a maximum of 65 by 1839, finally falling off markedly to 28 in 1851 and only 16 in 1852. The changing sample size compelled the use of percentages.

The duty of all reported engines was aggregated into seven classes: (i) those performing less than 20 million pounds raised one foot high by the consumption of a bushel of coals, (ii) 20 to 29·99 millions, (iii) 30 to 34·99 millions, (iv) 35 to 39·99 millions, (v) 40 to 49·99 millions, (vi) 50 to 59·99 millions, (vii) 60 millions and above. The number falling into each of these classes was expressed as a percentage of the total number reported in March of that year. As these particular classifications were arbitrary (though not meaningless, as shall be shown) and as the duty of many engines quite commonly changed by 5 per cent or more from one month to the next, the time profile of each class wavered erratically about its mean. Fluctuations from this cause and from the varying number of engines reported made some better method than observation by eye alone desirable. When the percentages were graphed over time, it was noticed that most of the classes roughly traced out upside-down parabolas. Because the derivation of turning points by graphical means has long been suspect, a regression of the percentages on a quadratic time function was carried out to date the year in which each class attained its greatest proportional representation on the average of all years. Thus if P_j was the percentage of total reported performances occurring in class j and

[1] Francis Trevithick, *Life of Richard Trevithick*, vol II, ch. 26 (London, 1872).

t was time (put equal to zero in 1811), one could estimate the coefficients of the quadratic equation as:

$$P_j = a_j + b_j t + c_j t^2 \qquad (1)$$

The following specifications were introduced:

(i) $b_j > 0$ A necessary condition for the maximum of P to be positive;

(ii) $c_j < 0$ This ensures the inverted parabola;

(iii) c_j was to be significant at the 5 per cent level of confidence, for if not the equation might be regarded as a mis-specification of the time distribution and the conclusions therefore untrustworthy.

It is an assumption of least-squares regression that the independent variables are uncorrelated with the error term. Thus one can derive:

$$\dot{P}_j = \frac{dP_j}{dt} = b_j + 2c_j t$$

and by elementary calculus the function reaches its maximum where $\dot{P} = 0$, i.e. where $t = -\dfrac{b}{2c}$. The second order condition for maximization is guaranteed by the sign specification on c. For the maximum to fall within the permissible period of observational data (1812–1852), $1 \leqslant t \leqslant 41$, so that $|2c| \leqslant b \leqslant |82c|$.

The results of the quadratic regressions for $j = 2, 3, \ldots 7$ (i.e. classes (ii) to (vii) inclusive) are shown in Table III:

Table III

Class	Years through which the regression was run	Coefficient of time	Coefficient of time squared	R^2	Year at which P a maximum
ii	1812–1839	0·954	− 0·1018	0·817	1815
iii	1812–1839	2·729	− 0·0892	0·638	1826
iv	1812–1852	1·437	− 0·0307	0·550	1834
v	1819–1852	3·218	− 0·0541	0·502	1840
vi	1826–1852	− 0·423	0·0312	0·615	—
vii	1826–1852	8·856	− 0·1503	0·743	1840

The time periods are truncated to avoid excessive influence of zero or insignificant tails to the distribution on the results. Alternative time periods were tried for some of the classes, but with little effect on the duty-maximizing year, given in the final column. Similarly, each series was smoothed by five-year moving averages and the regressions run again. Predictably, these regressions gave higher R^2's and lower Durbin-Watson statistics, i.e. greater positive autocorrelation,[1] but the results were once more quite robust. All coefficients satisfy the sign constraints except in the equation for class (vi), when neither coefficient is significant at acceptable levels anyway. Except for b_2, the coefficient of time in the second class, all estimates are significant at the 1 per cent level. The specification of permissible time range for maximum P is satisfied for all but the lowest class, which is therefore not shown in Table III.

The results can be interpreted in this way. The lowest class, of duties under 20 millions, is in decline before 1812, as the listless atmosphere of the first decade of the nineteenth century in Cornish mining gave way to the more enterprising spirit to which the Lean Reports themselves testify. Class (ii), duties of between 20 and 30 millions, peaked just at the introduction of the first of the important Woolf engines. These engines, employing steam of moderately high pressure, expanding it in one cylinder and condensing it in the same or a second cylinder, reached their maximum as a percentage of all engines in 1826. In that year engineers such as Samuel Grose instituted another jump in performances by improving steam jacketing and using sawdust to lag the steam pipes, taking expansion further, etc.

There is a climacteric following the height reached in the late 1830s, shown here by the apparently strange behaviour of the top two duty classes, and reflected in more general considerations, such as the decline in the number of engines submitted for reporting, and in the national interest taken in Cornish developments in such periodicals as the Transactions of the Institution of Civil Engineers. An explanation of the results obtained for these very high duties will be attempted at the end of this paper.

The short-period behaviour of duty increases therefore consists

---

[1] In the unsmoothed data, most Durbin-Watsons fall in the indeterminate range at the 5 per cent significance level. Considering the nature of the independent variables (pure time), this was regarded as satisfactory.

of a series of discontinuous jumps. For individual engines the
installation and 'learning' of the successive new techniques took
only a few months, but different engines were improved at
different times in the same manner to spread the diffusion process
over several years. In Diagram II, the performances of three
important engines are charted for each month from August 1827
to August 1829, during which each engine experienced a sharp
but pronounced rise in duty of around 20 millions.

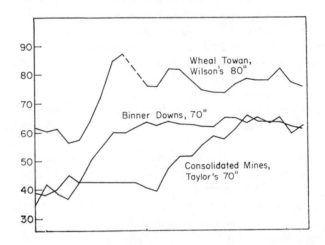

DIAGRAM II. Monthly duties of three major engines, August 1827
to August 1829.

In the longer term a more distinct trend can be established.
Thus while there were few outstanding technical advances during
the early 1820s, pit-work and equipment were strengthened and
the application of the pumping gear made more solid. Without
these the extended use of expansion in the later 1820s would have
been mechanically unbearable, in Farey's opinion.[1] A good fit to
the change through time of the maximum percentage use of
consecutive classes was given by a simple linear trend.[2] A plausible

[1] Farey, op. cit.
[2] The fitted equation was: Max P = 18·8 + 0·889 t, R^2 = 0·958. To obtain an adequate
number of observations, the number of classes was increased to twelve between 20 and
50 millions, taking each consecutive five and ten million duty interval, but using smoothed
data. The successive mid-points were then taken as the dependent variable, to give a time
scatter for 22·5, 25, 27·5, . . . , 50 millions.

reason for this upward drift of duty was that engine productivity rose to combat diminishing returns to real factor inputs in the given situation of ever-deepening mine shafts and increasing international competition (especially in copper). This explanation takes much for granted as will become evident, but there is some indirect substantiation.[1]

The nature of innovation makes a piecemeal engine-by-engine dating of the adoption of, say, greater expansion extremely difficult. And rather than resort to selecting a small number of engines for which the data might be adequate in the hope that the sample may be representative, we continue with the use of duty, the productivity index, as a surrogate for the introduction of new methods. In the March observations being used here, no Watt engine in pristine state burning highest-quality coals is ever known to have performed more than 35 millions. This level of duty is therefore chosen with some degree of confidence—taking a much higher cut-off point might mean neglecting instances of conversion of engines to the Cornish plan; while a much lower point might be attained by burning better-quality fuel. The dissemination of expansive working when coupled with steam-jacketing and superheating is thus studied by aggregating classes (iv) to (vii) above, i.e. all performances over 35 millions.

The diffusion of a new technology has frequently been suggested to be best approximated by the logistic curve.[2] This curve is asymptotic to zero and to the chosen ceiling value, and is symmetric around its centre, i.e. it takes on a leaning S-shape. A heuristic explanation might go as follows. Initially the new technique is in an experimental stage. The scope for its application can be known only at some cost. There may be considerable

---

[1] For example, product prices might be taken (subject to obvious reservations) as indices of profitability. The regression of average duty (see n. 3 on page 83) on copper and tin prices gave this result: $\bar{D} = 77.7 - 5.00 \, P_c - 1.33 \, P_t \qquad R^2 = 0.416$
$$(2.82) \qquad (0.92) \qquad R(P_c, P_t) = 0.684$$
The relatively high standard errors for each price variable are partly the consequence of a high intercorrelation between them, because of their susceptibility to similar kinds of fluctuations in demand. In view of the rather poor fit, conclusions must be guarded, but the coefficients show that a fall in prices (demand-induced?) tended to lead to a greater rise in average duties. If one can accept the idea of prices as a satisfactory surrogate for profits, it follows that falling profits rather than rising profits were responsible for technical progress quickening.

[2] *Locus classicus* in economic history is Zvi Griliches' application to the case of hybrid in the U.S.A. See particularly, 'Hybrid Corn: An Exploration in the Economics of Technological Change', *Econometrica* (Oct., 1957). For the general derivation used here see A. Lotka, *Elements of Physical Biology* (Baltimore, 1925).

resistance perhaps out of ignorance but also because its cost in relation to the advantage it brings is high. This resistance will be especially strong if to adopt the new method requires a substantial diversion of resources. If its adoption does, however, lead to significant economic gain, other firms in different cost situations or less favourably disposed to innovation will be induced to follow suit. The technique has now blossomed out of the experimental stage; its scope and perhaps its flexibility widen. More and more firms introduce it, until diminishing returns start to set in. Gradually a ceiling is approached at which all those firms that can benefit will have done so.

This explanation may over-specify or under-specify the requirements for the curve as actually applicable to the Cornish engine. It is not possible to verify whether any or all factors operated. A more systematic derivation of the logistic trend will, however, be rejected below.

In this example, the ceiling value is partly a function of the cut-off duty selected (the higher the duty, the lower the ceiling). For the duty of 35 millions, the ceiling value was first approximated by plotting the points on logistic graph paper, then later made more precise by choosing the best fit of alternative least-squares regressions. The ceiling was thereby established at 91 per cent. The logistic curve can then be formulated algebraically as:

$$P = 91/(1 + e^{m+nt}) \tag{2}$$

where m and n are the parameters to be estimated, and P and t the variables as before.

For regression purposes (1) is transformed to:

$$\frac{P}{91 - P} = e^{m+nt} \tag{2a}$$

Natural logarithms were taken and the curve fitted from 1816 (when P first became non-zero) to 1838, to give:

$$\log_e \frac{P}{91 - P} = -4 \cdot 402 + 0 \cdot 2516t \quad R^2 = 0 \cdot 931$$

The fitted curve, along with the actual observations, is plotted in Diagram III.

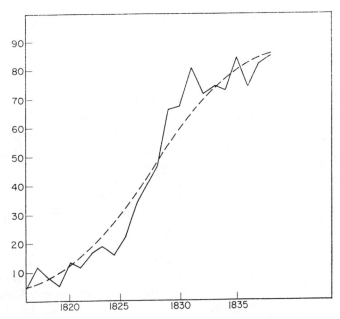

DIAGRAM III. Percentage of all reported engines performing at over 35 millions, 1816–38. Solid line: actual percentages (March of each year). Dashed line: percentages estimated from the logistic curve.

The high R^2 gave some strength to the belief that the logistic was appropriate description of the trend, but as Griliches has warned, it measures the fit of the transform (2a) and not P (as in (2)) itself. The estimated values of P, call them P*, were evaluated by substituting in the fitted curve for t and solving. 'Residuals' were then calculated as P* – P. A chart of these residuals showed, as indeed is obvious from Diagram III, that the logistic curve underrated the rate at which the improved practices were diffused during the central years 1825 to 1832.

It would be incorrect to suppose that because the steam engine was a large fixed item of capital investment, technical progress could be achieved only by being incorporated in new engines. Practically all the advances mentioned required at most the replacement of a small portion of the engine. For instance, Watt engines could be converted to high-pressure engines by strengthening the steam case and boilers, and modifying the valves. This phenomenon is still more marked for the later improvements—lagging the pipes, etc., involved no necessary interference with the machinery. If embodied technical progress is defined as by Johansen, where by implication the productivity of each machine (disregarding depreciation) is date-stamped on that machine at the time of its construction until demolition, then these new techniques did not have to be embodied in new engines.[1] Older vintages of engines did not have to be dismantled to make way. (In Diagram II, it will be observed that no break is discernible while the rapid increase takes place, although of course if the engine were out of work for a much shorter period than one month, its duty might still be reported. A new engine took, on the average, about two months to erect, not counting delivery time.[2])

Other definitions of embodiment are less exacting. If disembodied change consists solely of organizational change—'learning'—then pure disembodiment cannot account for a dominating proportion of the later improvements. In a paper read in 1824, Joseph Carne described at least eleven 'economical improvements which have nothing to do with the construction of the engine . . .' yet which bore upon its performance, ranging from altering the management of the fires (not building the fire too deep) to better cleaning of the engine.[3] Clearly most of the scope for advances of this kind had been worked out before the late 1820s. Yet the progress to come qualifies in most respects for Landes' class of 'anonymous technical change.'[4] The outlays involved were small; the rise in efficiency disproportionately great.

The thesis being advanced is that the relatively inconspicuous nature or even disembodiment of the technical changes accounts for their diffusion being unduly rapid. Along the fitted logistic

[1] L. Johansen, 'Substitution versus Fixed Production Coefficients in the Theory of Economic Growth: A Synthesis', *Econometrica* (April 1959). Seminal works on embodied technical progress include W. E. G. Salter, *Productivity and Technical Change* (2nd ed.) (Cambridge, 1966); and R. M. Solow, 'Investment and Technical Progress', in *Mathematical Methods in the Social Sciences*, ed. K. J. Arrow *et al.* (Stanford, 1960).

[2] Barton, op. cit., p. 130. Admittedly, a used engine could be re-erected more quickly than this, but the new engine will be the more appropriate comparison.

[3] In *Transactions of the Royal Geological Society of Cornwall*, vol. III (1828).

[4] David S. Landes, *The Unbound Prometheus* (Cambridge, 1969), ch. 2.

curve, the rate at which high-duty engines increase is governed by the number of engines already performing at high duty (to a quadratic approximation). In the case of engines on the Cornish plan, there is little doubt that the adoption of greater expansion, superheating, and the like, proceeded at a rate relatively unhindered by the weight of equipment operating under the previous technology with lower fuel economy.

Alternative explanations might be suggested for the fast rate of diffusion. It might have been simply the construction and reporting of an unprecedented number of large engines, which have been shown above to average consistently higher duties. In fact, the proportion of engines over 60 inches (cylinder diameter) appearing in the *Reporter* was exactly the same in 1832 as in 1825; while the ratio of engines of under 40 inches to those of 40 to 60 inches doubled over the same years.

Again, coal prices may have risen relative to the prices of other factor inputs sufficiently to have induced the exceptional rate of gain in fuel economy by dint of reducing the productivity of other factors, i.e. by moving along a stable production function. To test this, a coal price series was extracted from the ledgers of Harvey and Co. of Hayle,[1] who supplied Welsh coal to many mines in Southern Cornwall, notably to the great Wheal Vor mine, which at one time or another had eight separate pumping engines appearing in the Lean Reports, not to speak of a number of winding and stamping engines. In fact, average annual coal prices at Hayle fell sharply throughout the period of most rapid diffusion, 1826–32.[2] Alternative coal price series, incorporating (a) transport costs within Cornwall (based on the Wheal Vor accounts) and (b) lags in response, fared no better.

The economic theory, however, is based on relative factor prices, not absolute coal prices. The quantity of labour employed bore a virtually fixed relationship to the number of engines,[3] but as emerges from the observed relationships between engine size and duty, capital and coal were at least partly substitutable. Information on engine construction costs at present is very scarce, but the morsels available suggest that engine prices in 1823/4 were much the same as in 1834/5. In London the period 1826–32 saw

---

[1] Harvey's records are stored at the Cornwall C.R.O., Truro.

[2] Coal prices at Hayle fell steadily from 52s. 9d. in 1826 to 33s. 6d. per wey in 1831. This was easily the largest sustained reduction of the whole observation period (1813–1851).

[3] J. Bourne, *Treatise on the Steam Engine*, 1st. ed. (1856).

an extended trough in interest rates between the crash of 1825/6 and the recovery of 1833/6, with no obvious trend, while there were important institutional links, at least, between Cornwall and the London money market. It is conceivable that the tumble in market rates in 1825/6 gave some inducement to early experiments with clothing of steam pipes, etc., but there is no evidence for any continuation of such pressure as the number of high-duty engines rose above 30 per cent of all engines, nor any as duties in excess of, say, 60 millions began to be attained.

A second possibility is that 35-million-plus engines would have risen as a percentage of all engines at the expected logistic rate but for an abrupt improvement in the quality of coals consumed. Contemporary commentators leave us in no doubt that duty depended partly on the nature of the coal used, and supervised tests on individual engines strongly confirmed their judgement. The Cornwall coal price series derived above was divided through by the price of best coals in London.[1] Then the higher this ratio, the higher the quality of coals consumed in Cornwall and the more rapid the rise in duty that would be expected. But if this index does accurately depict the quality of Cornwall coal (it depends, for example, on assumptions made about relative shifts in demand and supply curves for different qualities of coals), then it gives the opposite result—so markedly inverse are the movements of this ratio and P from 1826 to 1831 that the inversity seems beyond generous allowance for error.

The years after 1838/9, by common consent of observers for the following half-century, saw the trend towards high duties recede. The class of highest duties, those of 60 millions and over, peaks in 1840, the same year as the crest of class (v) (40 and under 50 millions). Class (vi), 50–60 millions, reaches a local maximum in 1838/9, then drops back before advancing again very quickly after 1844. (This explains why the regression returned a positive coefficient on the time-squared term.)

Various causes have been brought forward for this decline. Some have attributed it to changes in the physical circumstances of pumping, especially more frequent resort to inclined shafts. But these problems had always existed: one can plausibly assert that on the production side, the role of technical progress of the kind described was to stave off diminishing returns to real factor

---

[1] In B. R. Mitchell with P. Deane, *Abstract of British Historical Statistics*, (Cambridge, 1962).

inputs into the mine. Barton has claimed that when the duty continuously exceeded 70 millions or so, the gain in fuel economy was more than offset by greater repair work from the additional strains on the machinery.[1] Yet improvements in castings and the invention of the riveting machine, etc., allowed much greater stresses to be imposed with safety. Through the spread of multiple compounding, surface condensation, and the like, the limits on duty figures attainable with the knowledge of engineering principles available in the 1840s was still some way ahead.

Others have thought the tapering off in duty the responsibility of poor management.[2] But there was no apparent exhaustion of engineering talent in Cornwall in the 1840s; and speculative managers had been known well before 1830.

These two suggestions are not refuted, but in the light of counter-objections seem quite minor alongside that of a decline in the quality of coals consumed after the late 1830s. Yet this fall in quality was not necessarily irrational. The duty figures, as I have shown, reflect performance per unit quantity of coal. Naturally a low-quality steam coal will always give a lower duty than coal of higher quality, but if the price ratios of the two qualities overcompensate for this deficiency, then on economic grounds the lower quality is clearly to be preferred. For example, in a footnote Barton mentions that:

'A 90″ Cornish engine at a London waterworks in 1864 gave 105m on coal costing 25s. 0d. per ton, a figure that was reduced to 65m using small coal costing 10s. 9d. per ton. In terms of cost rather than duty, the latter was thus more economical.'[3]

A manager will be indifferent between two qualities of coal for his engine if the ratio of the duties performed is proportional to their price ratio. This is why coal mines and other works in their immediate vicinity were able to run engines economically at low duty ratings, using small coals with very low market prices. Transport costs were governed largely by weight, not value of the coals being shipped. The upward shift of supply curves for differing qualities of coal was therefore roughly the same absolute amount for all qualities as distance from the coal-mine increased, but this meant a much larger proportional upward shift for

[1] Barton, op. cit., p. 59, quoting from the *West Briton.*
[2] W. J. Henwood summarizes the main arguments in his Presidential Address to the Spring Meeting of the Royal Institution of Cornwall in 1871.
[3] Barton, op. cit., p. 70n.

inferior qualities.[1] With no indigenous coal-mines, Cornwall was compelled to import all of its coal. But landing fees (lighterage, etc.) at the inadequate ports on the north-west coast of south Cornwall were high and internal transport within Cornwall very expensive. In 1835 the *Mining Journal and Commercial Gazette* estimated that on the average freight from quayside to mine in Cornwall added 7s. a ton to the quayside (landed) price of 18s. 6d.[2] High transport costs thus explain why Cornwall spearheaded technological advance to higher duties.

Similarly, reductions in freight rates, possibly for sea transport and certainly for internal carriage in Cornwall (the Hayle Railway, etc.) may help to explain the shift to lower quality coal in the 1840s. Farey, however, stressed the demand side.[3] In his view, the spread of steam navigation in the 1840s, for which the coal transport argument applied a fortiori, rapidly expanded the demand for high-quality coals, pushing up their price relative to the price of the middle quality. These hypotheses remain to be tested, but in the interim provide an entirely plausible explanation of observed technical developments from the late 1830s until the middle of the century.

[1] This result, that quality improves with distance from the source, has recently been derived theoretically. See J. P. Gould and Joel Segall, 'The Substitution Effects of Transportation Costs', *Journal of Political Economy* (Jan.–Feb. 1969). I am grateful to Professor S. Engerman of the University of Rochester for this reference and for considerable assistance in tightening the exposition at the last minute. For the structure and content I accept full responsibility.

[2] This figure appears to refer to the most important mining region, around Camborne and Redruth. This area was farthest from the coast and was whence most technical advances associated with the pumping engine originally stemmed. For mines of the St Ives district in 1841, average charges for transporting coal from quayside to mine were 4s. to 5s. per ton (J. S. Courtenay, 'Statistical Remarks on St Just in Penwith', *Reports of the Royal Cornwall Polytechnic Society*, vol. IX).

[3] Farey, op. cit., p. 260.

B

Essays in Social History

5

P. E. RAZZELL

Statistics and English Historical Sociology

I

Interesting examples of the use of statistics in studying historical sociology are to be found in the recent work of the Cambridge Group. Laslett has presented evidence to show that the nuclear family was the basic form of family structure in seventeenth century England, a finding which contradicts the conventional sociological generalization about industrialization destroying the extended family.[1] Similarly, Wrigley has published statistics of pre-marital conception rates in Colyton, Devon during the period from the late sixteenth century to the middle of the nineteenth,[2] which can be used to test generalizations about sexual habits in pre-industrial society and how they change over time. Wrigley found that the proportion of children conceived before marriage in Colyton had been 30 and 40 per cent during the seventeenth and eighteenth centuries, and had risen to over 50 per cent by the early nineteenth.[3] This type of evidence casts doubt on the popular sociological notion that pre-marital sexual relationships are of recent origin. It also contradicts the social historians' picture of the early nineteenth century as being a transitional period in the establishment of Victorian morality.

The major problem in the use of statistical data in the study of historical sociology is the unreliability of much of the evidence which forms the basis of the data. Laslett and Wrigley have both used original records in such a way as to be confident that their findings are reliable. In this essay I wish to illustrate the use of certain types of statistical sources which have been more or less

---

[1] P. Laslett, *The World We Have Lost* (1965), pp. 91–2. For a confirmation of this conclusion see the *1851 Census*, Vol. I, Table I, p. xliii.

[2] E. Wrigley, 'Family Limitation in Pre-Industrial England', *Economic History Review*, 2nd Series, Vol. XIX, No. 1, April 1966.

[3] A study recently published in *Population Studies* (Nov. 1966) showed that in a sample of 77 parishes the pre-marital conception rate was at least 20 per cent during the seventeenth century, rising to over 40 per cent during the eighteenth.

neglected, but are sufficiently reliable to test sociological hypotheses about English history. None of the findings presented are meant to be conclusive but are intended as illustrations of the way these sources may be used.

A much neglected source has been the marriage registers compiled after the introduction of civil registration. The following information was provided on each marriage certificate: (a) occupation of groom; (b) occupations of fathers of both groom and bride; (c) whether the groom and/or bride were able to sign their own names or not; (d) streets or places in which marriage partners were residing (sometimes); (e) age at marriage (sometimes). Using this type of information, a pilot study was carried out for All Saints Parish, Maidstone, for the period 1837–38,[1] and I shall briefly describe some of the sociological results of this study.

Two main subjects may be studied by using information from marriage certificates: social class differences and social mobility. The major problem in studying both subjects is how to establish criteria and define appropriate social classes, but it was possible to partially solve this problem by using some of the distinctions made in the register itself. Of a total of 115 grooms whose occupations were noted, 45 were registered as labourers, who tended to be a distinct and homogeneous sociological group, e.g. 17 of the 20 grooms who were living in Stone Street at the time of their marriage were labourers. The tendency for labourers to live in the same areas of the parish is confirmed by information from the 1841 census tracts for the town: both agricultural labourers and unskilled labourers working in the local paper-making factory and elsewhere tended to concentrate in special geographical clusters. The geographical distribution of different occupational groups is naturally quite complex in detail, with a general tendency towards overlapping. Some labourers lived in the same streets as skilled journeymen artisans (and occasionally with people of higher occupational status), who in their turn sometimes resided in the same streets as master artisans, tradesmen and professional people in other 'fringe' areas. However, the fact that 85 per cent of all grooms registered as residing in Stone Street (according to the Marriage Register) were labourers, indicates a sufficiently high concentration to treat labourers as a distinct residential group. They were also a relatively homogeneous group

---

[1] This marriage register is lodged in All Saints Church, Maidstone (Kent).

with respect to education; 22 of the 45 grooms who were labourers were unable to sign their own names in the marriage register, whereas this was true for only five of the 70 remaining grooms. This social class difference in education was also reflected in differences between different types of bride: 34 of the 45 brides marrying labourers were unable to sign their names, compared with only 13 of the remaining 70.

Although I have used geographical residence and education as criteria for defining social class, it would be technically more accurate to use them as criteria for what Weber called status groups, unless they were determining factors in the formation of the occupational groups (social classes are defined as essentially economic power groups). Weber's conception of the relationship between social classes and status groups was very complex, so I will attempt to briefly summarize in simplified form the apparent relationship implicit in his writings. Status groups may be seen as the social 'routinization' and stabilization of the much more dynamic and changing social classes; the stratification of status groups and social classes is likely to be identical during a historical period of little economic and social change (such as the European Middle Ages). Using a Weberian scheme of 'ideal type' analysis, we may say that during such a period there is a high degree of social homogeneity within social classes and a very insignificant amount of social mobility or exogamy between them. In order to test whether the labourers in Maidstone constituted a status group according to these criteria, it is not sufficient to know that they formed a relatively homogeneous group with reference to education and geographical residence, but it is also necessary to analyse the pattern of social mobility into and out of this class as well as the degree of endogamy practised.

In the Maidstone sample, 37 of the 45 grooms who were labourers were themselves sons of labourers, while 8 sons of 45 labourers had a different occupation from their fathers, indicating little social mobility into or out of this occupational group. This conclusion is confirmed by the fact that sons and daughters of labourers had approximately similar illiteracy rates as grooms who were labourers and their brides, i.e. education was a function of social class and not a factor fostering social mobility. There is information available in the Maidstone sample on the occupations of fathers of 44 brides who were married to labourers: 29 of these fathers were labourers themselves. As labourers only formed about 39 per cent of the sample of fathers, the proportion of labourers' brides marrying sons of labourers (about 66 per cent) is significantly greater than would be expected if marriage occurred randomly amongst the occupational groups, i.e. there was a relatively endogamous pattern of marriage amonst the Maidstone labourers. This occupational group formed a status group, in that it was characterized by a similar area of geographical residence, low social mobility and relative endogamy. Also the 'style of life' of labourers was distinctive in that they were illiterate to a much greater extent than other occupational groups.

The sociological distinction between unskilled labourers and skilled artisans is an important one for interpreting English social history. Contemporary observers such as Francis Place were aware of its importance for understanding differences in 'moral' attitudes and style of life. Henry Mayhew believed that 'the transition from the artisan to the labourer . . . is so great, that it seems as if we were in a new land, and among another race'. He believed that the difference between the two groups was significant in all respects, including politics, with the artisans being 'red-hot' radicals and the unskilled labourers being either apathetically unpolitical or for the 'maintenance of things as they are'. He cited the example of the operative tailors among whom 'there appeared to be a general bias towards the six points of the Charter' which contrasted markedly with the coal-whippers who 'were extremely proud of their having turned out to a man on the 10th of April, 1848, and become special constables for the maintenance of law and order on the day of the great Chartist demonstration'.[1] Hobsbawm has recently emphasized this distinction in his discussion of the labouring aristocracy. Skilled artisans received twice the wages of unskilled labourers, and were sufficiently respectable to merit the appellation of 'lower-middle class' on certain occasions.[2] The association between the lower-middle class of artisans and small tradesmen and puritanism, with all that it implied for political radicalism, was strong as early as the seventeenth century.[3] The linking of artisans with small tradesmen was recognized as valid by the Registrar-General in 1838 when

---

[1] H. Mayhew, *London Labour and the London Poor* (1861), Vol. 3, p. 233.
[2] E. J. Hobsbawm, *Labouring Men* (1964), pp. 273–4.
[3] The best statistical evidence for this conclusion is to be found in W. A. Cole, *The Quakers and Politics 1652–1660* (University of Cambridge Thesis 1955), pp. 302–318.

statistics of suicide rates in London were published: labourers—
2·9 suicides per 10,000 males (20 years and above) living; artisans
and tradespeople—6·0 per 10,000.[1] This emphasis on the distinction between artisans and labourers does not mean that it was the
most important class difference during this period and it is
clear that other equally valid distinctions can be made, e.g.
Mayhew also noted the marked income and educational differences between 'society' (trade union) artisans and those working
in a ruthlessly competitive situation under the 'sweated' conditions
of their own garrets. E. P. Thompson has recently argued that a
new type of working class solidarity, cutting across manual
occupational boundaries, emerged during the first half of the
nineteenth century. A more revealing analysis of class structure is
that made by Foster in his recent work,[2] which is based on a
modified Marxist theoretical framework. Foster has made a
distinction between Oldham with an economy dominated by a
small number of very big firms, and Northampton where there
were a large number of small firms. In Oldham the social distance
between skilled and unskilled workers was small whereas in
Northampton it was significantly greater. Foster has measured
social distance by using the indices of inter-marriage and neighbourhood residence patterns, statistics of which he has compiled
from local marriage registers and census documents. He has also
linked the structure of status groups with the nature of class
consciousness and conflict groups (what Weber called 'Party'),
although there are formidable methodological problems involved
in measuring 'class consciousness'.

A thorough analysis of the social structure of Maidstone would
involve a systematic analysis of social mobility, inter-marriage,
educational and neighbourhood residence patterns by occupational
group, linked with other appropriate evidence about styles of
life, as well as political activity. The latter type of evidence is
almost certainly going to be of a literary kind, except where poll-
book information is available (this is likely to be rare for groups
such as labourers).[3] There is the additional difficulty of being unable
to distinguish from census records (and the like) real sociological

---

[1] *3rd Annual Registrar-General's Report*, 1841, p. 79.
[2] In H. J. Dyos (Ed.) *The Study of Urban History* (1968).
[3] Since this article was written Vincent has written his book *Pollbooks: How Victorians
Voted* (1967) which shows that Maidstone labourers voted consistently more Con-
servative than did craftsmen.

differences between occupations which are listed in identical manner but may in fact be very different, e.g. a 'tailor' may be a master employing several men (the 1851 census was supposed to have noted this but did not always do so), a skilled journeyman working in a superior workshop (Mayhew's 'society' man), a semi-skilled member of a tailoring sweat-shop, or a garret-master working under 'sweated' domestic conditions. The incomes of these groups are known to have been very different, and it is questionable whether they ought to be put together in the same class category.

In the analysis of the Maidstone data, I have restricted the discussion to the sociological differences between labourers and other occupational groups; this is mainly due to the nature of the data itself, i.e. the social homogeneity of the Maidstone labourers became clear from even a cursory examination of the statistical evidence, which was not true for other occupations. It is possible, however, to assess to some extent the social mobility pattern for the total Maidstone sample. Of 115 grooms, 65 had the same occupations as their fathers, while a further 11 had the same occupations as their fathers-in-law. It is difficult to measure total social mobility for this group, as there are no readily available criteria to distinguish the social status of the different occupations. A somewhat arbitrary method is to divide the sample of grooms into two equal groups: 57 unskilled as against 58 skilled and others. The unskilled includes all the labourers plus 6 servants, 4 bricklayers and 2 watermen, while the skilled includes all the artisans (such as papermakers and carpenters), tradesmen and professional people, as well as one or two dubious cases such as army privates. Support for this division is provided by the fact that the occupations of the non-labouring grooms who were illiterate were: one servant, bricklayer, waterman, army private and basket-maker (a total of 5 cases). On this basis of social division of occupations, of the total 115 cases, 5 grooms achieved a 'higher' position than their fathers, as against 16 whose occupational status was 'lower'. This result is not surprising during a period of rapid population increase in an area outside of industrial expansion, where most upward social mobility took place. Any index of total social mobility, e.g. $18\frac{1}{2}$ per cent of men crossing the two social classes, would be misleading as the basis of comparison with more recent experience, because of differences in social structure and the questionable validity of such an index.[1] A more appropriate comparison is that for specific occupational groups: about 82 per cent of the groom labourers in Maidstone were the sons of labourers, whereas the comparable figure for the cohort of unskilled occupations in Glass's twentieth century sample was about 40 per cent.[2] This suggests a significant increase in social mobility but is only suggestive because the two samples are not directly comparable. It is clear, however, that social mobility must have been low during the earlier period, which is associated with the high proportion of Maidstone sons who followed their fathers' occupations.

It is possible that there was a greater amount of social mobility in areas other than Maidstone—particularly in industrial regions—and during the pre-industrial period before the economic polarization associated with capitalism had developed. Richard Baxter in his book on the *Poor Husbandman* written during the latter part of the seventeenth century, noted how easy it was for agricultural labourers to set themselves up as small tenant farmers, although the economic and social benefits from this step do not appear to have been large. It is well known how relatively easy it was for journeymen weavers to set themselves up as small independent clothiers in areas such as Yorkshire before the emergence of the capitalist factory system. It is obviously desirable that such forms of social mobility be statistically measured, but unfortunately there is a great paucity of reliable information. One possible source is the Anglican marriage licences which sometimes give the occupations of both grooms and their fathers. The Sussex marriage licences for the period 1755–1800 are particularly good for the information they give; of 60 cases sampled, 44 fathers and sons were listed as having the same occupations.[3] The proportion of sons and fathers having the same occupation was slightly higher in this Sussex sample than it is in that from Maidstone. This suggests that there was no significant amount of social mobility in rural areas during the pre-industrial period, although it is possible that the enclosure movement, etc., had affected

---

[1] Lipset and Bendix used such an index in their comparative study of social mobility in industrial societies; their index is particularly questionable as it does not allow for distinction between upward and downward social mobility. See S. M. Lipset and R. Bendix, *Social Mobility in Industrial Society* (1959), pp. 25, 26, 72.

[2] D. V. Glass (ed.), *Social Mobility in Britain* (1953), p. 187.

[3] D. Macleod (ed.), Calendar of Sussex Marriage Licences, *Sussex Record Society*, Vols. XXXII and XXXV.

Sussex sufficiently by 1755–1800 to diminish the kind of mobility described by Baxter. It is also possible that intra-generational social mobility was much more frequent than the form of inter-generational mobility (between fathers and sons) that we have been measuring. There is no evidence available on this for the earlier period, and only a fragment of information for the mid-nineteenth century. Williams has studied the census records of the West Country village of Ashworthy for the years 1841 and 1851.[1] According to his published statistics, in a village of a population just over 1,100, only two men who were labourers in 1841 were farmers by 1851, whereas two families whose heads were farmers in 1841 had become paupers by 1851 (the heads of the families dying in the intervening period).[2] This finding indicates little intra-generational social mobility, which confirms the other statistical evidence which we have considered for the period before the mid-nineteenth century.

The discussion of sociological statistics in the study of English history has been mainly confined in this paper to evidence derived from marriage registers kept under the civil registration system and lists of special marriage licences issued by the Anglican Church. This raises the question as to how accurate these marriage records were with reference to the sociological information contained in them. It is partially possible to check the accuracy of the Anglican special licences by comparing some of their information with that in parish registers (this is also a cross-check on the reliability of the parish register). Some of the Sussex licences give the period of residence in the parish from which a person was married. In the cases where this was 'all his (or her) lifetime', it is possible to check back in the parish register to see whether they were actually born in the parish, and whether the age at marriage given in the licences is accurate. This was done for 40 persons married by licence issued in the Chichester Archdeaconry during the period 1760–1800.[3] Only two of these 40 persons could not be traced in the parish register, no mention being made of their family during the estimated period of their births. Thus both the parish register and the marriage licences are relatively accurate as records in respect to when and where a person was born and how

[1] W. M. Williams, *A West Country Village Ashworthy* (1963).
[2] Ibid., p. 128.
[3] Macleod, op. cit.

long they had lived in the parish before marriage. The ages at marriage are somewhat less in agreement in the comparison between parish register and marriage licence. Of the 38 traced cases, there was approximate agreement in 22, a difference of about one year in nine, and somewhat greater differences in the remaining seven cases. All but one of the differences were due to the understatement of age in the marriage licences, but such differences are not large enough to significantly affect median ages at marriage calculated from the two types of data (age stated in the licences and reconstituted age at marriage from the parish register).

The information in the Sussex licences enables us to compile statistics of the relative geographical mobility of different occupational groups.

Table 1

PROPORTION OF PEOPLE LIVING IN SUSSEX PARISHES FOR ALL THEIR LIFE BEFORE MARRIAGE[1]

Groom's Occupation	Period	Per cent 'All Their Lives'			
		Grooms %	N	Brides %	N
Labourers	1786–1800	2	100	18	100
All Occupations	1793–1794	16	100	24	100
Farmers and Yeomen	1790–1797	46	100	39	100

The variations in geographical mobility were much greater amongst grooms than brides. The difference between labourers and farmers was most marked: two as against 46 per cent living all their lives until marriage in their parish of birth. This result should not surprise us, for most farmers and yeomen (as opposed to 'husbandmen') probably owned some of their own land which would tend to tie them to particular parishes, whereas labourers owning no land had to move to areas where cottages and remunerative work was available. This is reflected in literary evidence, e.g. the description of the hire at local farms of labourers for the year. Presumably women were more likely to live all their lives until marriage in their parish of birth as there was less economic necessity for them to move, although this was not true of domestic servants.

[1] Ibid.

The occupational differences in geographical mobility have been studied by Williams in his analysis of the 1841 and 1851 census records of Ashworthy. He has studied both immigration and emigration from the parish during this decade.

Table 2

INTERCENSAL MOVEMENT OF (ASHWORTHY) POPULATION 1841–1851[1]

	Farmers' Families	Craftsmen's Families	Labourers' Families	Other
IMMIGRATION				
Living in same dwelling	161	76	115	66
Moved within Ashworthy	42	32	102	34
Came to Ashworthy	19	27	123	38
Changed status	10	—	—	—
Children born in Ashworthy	71	55	101	23
Total 1851	303	190	441	161
EMIGRATION				
Living in Ashworthy (1841 and 1851)	213	108	317	
Probably moved from Ashworthy	64	31	202	
Died	21	11	73	
Changed status	9	—	—	
Not known	—	11	36	
Total 1841	307	161	628	

These statistics confirm our conclusions that farmers were very much less geographically mobile than labourers, and this was true even for movement within the parish itself. However, it is possible to produce statistics for other parishes to show that labourers had lower mobility rates than the general population,[2] and this is a subject that can only be settled after very much more research.

The statistics of geographical mobility so far considered suggest that the traditional picture of stable English village communities in which inhabitants lived their whole lives, is incorrect. This point is sociologically important as sociologists have too easily assumed that the pre-industrial English village formed a 'Gemeinschaft' type of community, with the sense of community based on

[1] Williams, op. cit., p. 128.
[2] For example, in Harlow, Essex (1851), labourers formed about a third of the resident natives but only about a fifth of people not born in the parish.

life-long face-to-face social contact within the context of a closed system of social relationships. The 'Gemeinschaft' community arises when sociability is structured between individuals for a major part of their lifetime (in the extreme case for the whole of their lifetime). One way of studying this subject is to examine the proportion of any village population which has lived in that village since birth. According to Williams's statistics for Ashworthy, just over 72 per cent of the 1851 population were born in the village;[1] this figure includes children as well as adults, which would tend to be higher than the proportion just for adults. This is reflected in Williams's findings, for amongst adults 67·8 per cent of farmers, 59·6 per cent of male farm workers and servants and 62·5 per cent of female farm servants were born in Ashworthy.[2] These proportions are still surprisingly high, in the light of the movements of the population into the village between 1841 and 1851; if we exclude children born in the parish during this decade, about a quarter of the 1851 population had moved into the village during the ten-year period. It is therefore surprising that such a high proportion of adults were listed as having been born in the village, although there is no necessary contradiction between the two types of evidence. It is possible that many families (particularly those of labourers) moved to several parishes before coming back to their home parish. Evidence for this is to be found in the 1851 census documents, e.g. Jonathan Foster, a labourer, was born in Latton, Essex, and his wife Sarah was born in Harlow, Essex; their first five listed children were born in Latton, but the last two were born in Harlow, where the whole family was enumerated in 1851. Much of the migration into and out of Ashworthy might have been of this type and would explain the high proportion of people listed as having been born in the parish. Another factor of some importance explaining the discrepancy between the statistics of migration and 'nativity' is the greater number of emigrants than immigrants—much of the geographically mobile population found its way into large towns rather than other villages, thus diminishing the proportion of 'foreigners' in any one village. It is therefore possible that there was more geographical mobility between villages (and therefore lower proportions of native populations in these villages) during

[1] Williams, op. cit., p. 123.
[2] Ibid.

the pre-industrial period and in fact this does seem to have been the case, e.g. of the 401 people living in Clayworth in 1676, only 158 were still living there in 1688, 91 dying in the parish during the intermediary period.[1] However, other types of evidence suggest that there was no significant increase in geographical mobility, e.g. see Table 3.

Table 3

PROPORTION OF PEOPLE MARRYING IN COLYTON, DEVON, WHO WERE BORN IN THE PARISH[2]

Period	Number of Marriages	Number married and born in the parish		Per cent	
		Men	Women	Men	Women
1560–1646	854	258	371	30	43
1647–1719	379	109	136	29	36
1720–1769	424	90	104	21	25
1770–1837	888	219	275	25	31

Although the English rural population was geographically mobile as early as the late sixteenth century, most of this mobility was probably restricted to a group of local parishes. There is no systematic statistical evidence for this conclusion for the earlier period, and only a limited amount for the later one. According to the 1841 population census, 80·7 per cent of the English population were born in the county that they were living in at the time of the census, and Williams concluded from his study of the 1851 census records of Ashworthy that most of the immigrants into the village were born within the area of a ten-mile radius of the parish.[3] This confirms what we know about the area in which migration occurred from the study of settlement certificates, as well as conclusions reached from an examination of particular family histories, e.g. the surname Dilnot was confined to a group of East Kent parishes, within a circle of a 20 mile radius, from as early as the fourteenth century through to the nineteenth.[4]

Not only was the rural population very much more mobile than has been commonly assumed, but the inhabitants of large towns seem to have moved very frequently from one house to another within the town itself.

[1] P. Laslett and J. Harrison, 'Clayworth and Coganhoe', in H. E. Bell and R. L. Ollard (eds.), *Historical Essays 1600–1750* (1963), p. 174.
[2] Wrigley, op. cit.
[3] Williams, op. cit., p. 123.
[4] I am grateful to Mr R. Dilnot for this information.

Table 4

LENGTH OF TIME WHICH THE HEADS OF FAMILIES HAVE RESIDED IN
THEIR PRESENT DWELLINGS

(St. George's-in-the-East, 1848)[1]

	Families	Single Men	Single Women	Total Families
1–4 weeks	60	3	2	65
1–6 months	369	10	12	391
6 months–1 year	270	17	13	300
1–3 years	467	18	12	497
3–6 years	269	8	6	283
6–9 years	148	3	—	151
9–12 years	69	—	4	73
Over 12 years	136	2	7	145
Not ascertained	14	27	8	49
	1,802	88	64	1,954

This table summarizes a survey conducted by the Royal Statistical Society amongst the poor of St. George's-in-the-East, London, in 1848. The median period of residence for all families was about two years, a very short period of time compared to the lengthy periods spent in particular houses according to current surveys of working class populations such as that in Bethnal Green. In fact it is possible to make some kind of comparison of geographical mobility patterns in Bethnal Green at the middle of the nineteenth and twentieth centuries. According to a survey carried out by Glass and Frankel in 1944 seventy-seven per cent of the heads of families were born in the borough of Bethnal Green; a sample of 100 adults residing in Temple Street, Bethnal Green, in 1851 had an equivalent figure of 25 per cent, i.e. 25 of them had been born in the parish. Of course these figures are not strictly comparable, but they probably suggest the significant difference between the two periods fairly accurately, and indicate the kind of historical comparisons that can be made with this type of data.[2]

The reasons for the high amounts of geographical mobility within places like St. George's-in-the-East and Bethnal Green during the mid-nineteenth century are not hard to find. Their

[1] See the *Journal of the Royal Statistical Society*, Vol. XI (1848).
[2] One working-class informant in the early 1950s could not remember anyone moving into the street of seventy houses in which he lived (in Bethnal Green) during a forty-year period. See J. H. Robb, *Working Class Anti-Semite* (1954), p. 57, for this and other information about geographical mobility in Bethnal Green.

total population was expanding very rapidly during the nine-teenth century, e.g. the population of the borough of Bethnal Green multiplied by about six times during the second quarter of the nineteenth century[1]—as the indigenous population was expanding at a very much slower rate, most of the increase came from immigration into the area. It is possible that other factors played a part in the very high turnover in house occupation in a place like St. George's-in-the-East: the need to move near new employment (transport being very inadequate) or the frequent evictions of the poor from their homes because of their inability to always pay the rent (this latter factor may have played a major part in the village of Ashworthy where the other factors are not likely to have played such an important part). Much of the mobility so far discussed took place within a relatively small area so that many of the immigrants into Temple Street, Bethnal Green, for example, came from neighbouring parishes of Shore-ditch and St. Lukes. However, many of the sample came from outside London, a fact which is also reflected in the statistics of 'nativity' for London as a whole: of the 1·4 million adults living in London in 1851, about a half had been born outside the city. In fact this is a relatively high proportion compared with the relevant statistics of other towns during the same period: of Manchester and Salford's adult population of 226 thousand only just over one quarter were born in the city. Even very small towns like Dorchester, Dorset (adult pop. 3,734), Truro, Cornwall (adult pop. 6,161) and Bedford (adult pop. 6,354) had very low proportions of resident adult natives: 32 per cent, 38 per cent and 28 per cent. A place like Birmingham with an adult population of 127 thousand in 1851 had a higher proportion of natives: 44 per cent.[2] This proportion was higher than that found in some small villages, e.g. the parish of Havering, Essex (adult pop. 233), had only 11 per cent adult native residents.[3] Mere size was not the only factor in determining the proportion of native residents; the economy of a particular town, the demand for labour from the countryside, etc., would all determine the pattern of geographical mobility. Havering, Essex, probably had such a small proportion of native residents because it was so near London, which drew

[1] Ibid., p. 195. According to census data the population of Bethnal Green district quadrupled between 1801 and 1851.
[2] For all these statistics of nativity see *1851 Census*, Vol. 1, Population Tables 2, p. 418.
[3] See the 1851 Census documents for Havering in the Public Record Office.

much of its population from the surrounding countryside. London itself was big enough to provide work for all its native residents, who might have to move from parish to parish, but would still be able to find work and housing somewhere within the city. Villages relatively isolated from large towns appear to have had a large proportion of resident natives, e.g. of Garsington, Oxon's 327 adult population, 70 per cent had been born in the village according to the 1851 Census.[1] Garsington is thus like Ashworthy in its high proportion of native residents; an example of an 'intermediate' village is Harlow, Essex, of whose 275 adult population (1851), 39 per cent had been born there.[2]

It is clear that we cannot assume that agricultural villages were necessarily Gemeinschaft villages—many had relatively mobile populations who had not shared socially structured relationships for the major part of their lifetimes. This provisional conclusion is logically related to findings about the structure of the family and the relationship between neighbourhood and kinship. Willmott and Young found that the 'extended family' is common in traditional Bethnal Green, but this is the case only because the population is so static. If there is little migration into or out of a community, a network of kinship relationships is bound to be built up (unless the population is decreasing rapidly). This may be illustrated by the case of Garsington where the same surname exists much more frequently than it does in Maidstone during the same period; of a sample of 100 listed names of heads of households taken from the 1851 Census in both places, the most frequent name (Quartermaine) was mentioned nine times in Garsington as against only three (King) in Maidstone. This is what one would expect as the former place had 70 per cent resident adult natives while the latter had only 36 per cent.[3] This is not the only factor determining kinship neighbourhood patterns, as even if a population was geographically mobile it could still migrate with other members of the family.

It is partly possible to measure the geographical mobility patterns of family members from information in the Sussex licences. When a person getting married was under 21 they needed their parents' consent and the places of residence of child and parent were given. Of 100 grooms, 42 were residing (during the

[1] See the 1851 Census document for Garsington in the Public Record Office.
[2] 1851 Census documents for Harlow in the Public Record Office.
[3] *1851 Census*, Vol. 1, Population Tables 2, p. clxxiii.

latter half of the eighteenth century) in the same parish as their
parents at the time of marriage; the comparable figure for brides
is 80 out of 100. Thus brides were much more likely than grooms
to live in the same parish as their parents, although they may have
subsequently moved more frequently to their husband's present
parish where he presumably worked. There were significant
differences amongst different occupational groups for the grooms:
all 12 farmers and yeomen in the sample lived in the same parish
as their parents, whereas this was true for only four of 24 labourers,
none of 28 husbandmen (tenant farmers), but as many as eight of
ten artisans.[1] These findings confirm those about class differentials
in geographical mobility for the Sussex sample and suggest that
economic factors were most important in determining the relationship between kinship and neighbourhood. The whole
question of neighbourhood and kinship patterns is clearly very
complex, as is the related theme of geographical mobility. Only
after much further research into community and class differences
will it be possible to make confident generalizations. What is
certain is the influence of population and economic growth on the
mobility and kinship neighbourhood patterns. It was possible
for kin to cluster in the same neighbourhoods in Bethnal Green
because of the relatively static population and economic position
of the area during the first half of the twentieth century. Much of
this population was moved during the 1950s and '60s as the result
of a planning decision to 'improve' the area and rehouse willing
migrants in Greenleigh and elsewhere, and this was when many
married children were separated from their parents who stayed
behind in the old community (the proportion of older people
surviving in a community is also obviously important in determining this type of relationship). Perhaps the type of geographical
mobility which separates kin will increase as social mobility is
fostered by the spread of education, although this factor itself
could become relatively stabilized in time, as did the population
and economic changes in places like Bethnal Green during the
late nineteenth century.

There are one or two other historical sociological topics which
may be briefly illuminated through the use of unfamiliar statistical
sources. It is possible to calculate the age of marriage of different
social groups as early as the eighteenth century.

[1] Macleod, op. cit.

Table 5

MEDIAN FIRST AGE AT MARRIAGE IN SUSSEX[1]

Period (approx.)	Labourers		All Occupations		Yeomen Farmers	
	Grooms	Brides	Grooms	Brides	Grooms	Brides
1757–69	25½	23	26½	23½	27	24
1788–1800	24	22	25	22½	25½	23

(each median was calculated from a sample of 100 cases)

In late eighteenth-century Sussex there was about one year's difference in the median age at first marriage between labourers and other occupational groups; this was true for both grooms and brides (although the difference is greater amongst grooms than brides). There is very little alternative evidence to check this finding; a brief analysis of the Nottinghamshire marriage licences yielded no significant difference in the age at marriage between different occupational groups. The age at first marriage differed between the two social classes defined for Maidstone: during 1837/38, of the 57 brides marrying grooms with unskilled occupations, 18 married below the age of 21, as compared to only 10 of the remaining 58 brides. Thus the Maidstone marriage statistics tend to confirm those for Sussex, although it does appear that the class differential in the age at marriage was widening throughout the nineteenth century: certainly the age at first marriage was rising amongst the aristocracy during the nineteenth century,[2] whilst among the total population it probably did not change much on average (this could mask changes between social classes, e.g. the age of marriage amongst the middle classes might have risen, whilst that among the working class fallen). Again further research is needed to settle this issue, particularly as it might have some bearing on the relationship between the age at marriage and the practice of birth control amongst the different social classes and how these factors changed over time.

Finally, there is one other subject which may be profitably studied through a neglected statistical source: attendance at communion service. The Anglican incumbents of Tenterden in Kent, noted the number of communicants during the main religious festivals for the period 1731–1848, although there are

[1] Ibid.
[2] T. H. Hollingsworth, *The Demography of the British Peerage* (supplement to Population Studies, Vol. XVIII, no. 2, pp. iv and 108, 205).

long gaps in the record.[1] I shall confine the discussion to the number of Easter communicants, as it reflects quite accurately the numbers of those at other times of the year, and the following table represents the predominant trends throughout the whole period.

Table 6

THE NUMBERS OF EASTER COMMUNICANTS IN TENTERDEN, 1731–1848

Date:	1731	1756	1761	1774	1781	1809	1848
No. of communicants	140	142	239	250	230	140	124

The number of communicants was more or less constant between 1731 and 1756, after which it rose very sharply. It is difficult to explain the rise between 1756 and 1761, as the number of baptisms fell slightly during the same period and only began to rise from 1763 onwards, which probably reflected an increase in population. The number of communicants reached a final peak in 1774, after which it began to fall slightly. Between 1781 and 1809 there is a complete blank in the record, and the figure for 1809 is markedly smaller than that for 1781. There were large fluctuations after this, although the final figure for 1848 was somewhat smaller than that for 1809. This decline in the number of communicants during the first half of the nineteenth century is all the more remarkable in the context of an expanding population: it increased from 2,370 in 1801 to 3,782 in 1851. The main decline in the number of communicants, however, appears to have occurred between 1780 and 1809, and although there are no population figures available for this period it is possible to express communicants as a proportion of baptisms. This proportion changed from just over 4:1 in 1731 to 5:1 in 1781, dropping sharply to under 2:1 by 1809. Making certain standard assumptions about the birth rate and the age structure of the population, we may estimate that about 40 per cent of the eligible population were communicants before 1780 and only about 10 per cent by 1848.

Some of the changes in the proportion of the eligible population who were communicants might be due to the policy of particular incumbents but this can hardly explain the long term trend. It is possible that some of the decline can be attributed to the emergence of Methodism during the relevant period. In 1790, Hastep estimated that there were in Tenterden, '2,000 inhabitants, of

[1] See the Tenterden parish register, lodged in the Kent County Record Office.

which about 500 were dissenters, who have two meeting houses here, one of Presbyterians, the other of Methodistical Baptists.[1] According to the religious census of 1851, there were in the Tenterden district (an area covering Tenterden and several surrounding villages) 7,412 total sittings, of which 2,650 belonged to dissenters. The increase in the proportion of dissenters—from about 25 per cent in 1790 to 35 per cent in 1851—cannot explain the degree of decline in the number of Anglican communicants in relation to the increase of population. There is no obvious explanation for this decline, and it might simply reflect the customary abandonment of ritual participation in Anglican services just in the town of Tenterden. Some contemporaries did note the religious apathy of agricultural labourers and Engels quoted the labourers who told a journalist in 1843 that they only went to Church because of it being a condition of receiving work and charitable concessions of fuel and potato plots.[2] It is possible that the creation of a landless agricultural proletariat through the enclosure movement may have destroyed the 'organic' sense of solidarity the poor are supposed to have felt with the rich before the enclosure movement, but this type of explanation involves an analysis of the changing social structure of Tenterden which it is not possible to pursue here. One specific factor might have been of some influence: the elimination of smallpox at the end of the eighteenth century. There was a general inoculation in the town in 1798 which appears to have covered all the vulnerable population; it is possible that the elimination of the great killer disease of smallpox removed one of the psychological reasons for religious worship (the early clerical opponents of inoculation predicted that it would have this effect): fear of death and disease.[3] Whatever the reasons for the decline of religious participation during the first half of the nineteenth century, it is clear that such a finding contradicts the conventional picture of this being a period of religious revival. Like the increase in Colyton pre-marital conception rate, the fall in the number of Tenterden communicants leads us to question historical generalization based purely upon literary evidence.

[1] E. Hasted, *The History of the County of Kent* (Canterbury, 1790), p. 98.
[2] F. Engels, *The Condition of the Working Class in England* (1958), pp. 303, 304.
[3] An example of the effect of disease on religious behaviour is the trebling of church and chapel communitants during and after the chlorea epidemic of 1849 in Merthy Tydfil. See *The Morning Chronicle* 15.4.50.

Practically all the statistical data in this paper has been about very specific localities, and England is a country with a history notorious for its regional variations. A great deal more research will have to be done before it is possible to make confident generalizations about any subject discussed in this paper, but as a great wealth of the relevant information is to be found in the Registrar-General's vaults and Public Record Office's ledgers, perhaps we can expect social historians and historical sociologists to do the sort of research required to reach definitive conclusions. No doubt many historical myths will wither in the process, possibly to be replaced by new ones in innocent statistical clothing. There are limits to the usefulness of statistics: how inadequate numbers are in describing the fact that six people died of starvation in Riseley, Bedfordshire, during the period 1690–1742,[1] but although these deaths are only casually recorded they do at least warn us against the myth of the pre-industrial golden age.

[1] See the Riseley Parish Register, *Bedfordshire Parish Registers*, XXVIII, in the Bedfordshire Record Office.

6

M. E. ROSE

The New Poor Law in an Industrial Area

I

'This reform must ever be regarded as in the first rank of the honours of the Whig administration and of the pregnant victories of the peace', wrote Harriet Martineau of the Poor Law Amendment Act of 1834.[1] Many of her contemporaries were less fulsome in their praise of that measure, and their attitude has been shared by historians. Mark Blaug has recently shown that the 1834 Report of the Royal Commission on the Poor Laws, on which the Act of 1834 was based, made no attempt to analyse the bulky evidence which the Commission had amassed.[2] Not only was the Report 'wildly unhistorical', it was also utterly unstatistical. The legislators, in their turn, ignored or watered down many of the recommendations of the Report. After 1834, a weak and divided central authority failed in its attempt to abolish many of the abuses of the old poor law system such as the granting of outdoor relief to the able-bodied poor or the 'general mixed' workhouse.[3] Nowhere was this failure more apparent than in the industrial districts of the North of England. Economic historians have frequently pointed out that the reforms prescribed by the Royal Commission had little hope of succeeding in the industrial areas. The workhouse test was largely irrelevant to the problems of cyclical unemployment. This fact, together with the violent movement of protest which greeted the extension of the New Poor Law to the manufacturing districts of Lancashire and the

---

[1] H. Martineau, *History of the Thirty Years' Peace* (1877 Ed.) Vol. ii, p. 512.
[2] M. Blaug, 'The Poor Law Report Re-examined', *Journal of Economic History*, xxiv (1964), pp. 229–45.
[3] For a full account: S. & B. Webb, *English Local Government: English Poor Law History: Part II. The Last Hundred Years* (2 vols., 1929). (Subsequently referred to as 'Webb'); S. E. Finer, *The Life and Times of Sir Edwin Chadwick* (1952).

West Riding in 1837, prevented the application of the harsher aspects of the new system in these areas.[1]

Such an interpretation is substantially correct, and it is not the intention of this essay to amend it significantly. The workhouse test was not, however, the only question at issue between the local authorities in the North and the Poor Law Commission, nor was the opposition to the New Poor Law in the North confined to the turbulent but brief career of the Anti Poor Law Movement, the mass of whose support had faded away into the wider Chartist Movement within two years of its formation. Recent local studies of the Poor Law in the North during the 20 or 30 years following the extension of the New Poor Law machinery to the area have shown the importance of other sources of opposition to the new system and revealed additional reasons for its failure to develop into anything but a pale shadow of what its framers intended.[2] The belief that the industrial parishes of the North had already reformed their system of poor law administration before 1834, the intense hostility to interference by a central authority, the resistance to any change in the system of relief, together with the failure of the New Poor Law to reform the laws of settlement or the financial basis of the poor law, all contributed to the failure of the New Poor Law in the industrial North. It is the purpose of this essay to examine these factors in as much detail as space makes possible.

The passage of the Poor Law Amendment Bill through Parliament in 1834 was regarded with a surprising degree of

[1] Vide, for example: A. Redford, *The Economic History of England, 1760–1860* (2nd Edition, 1960), pp. 121–2.

J. D. Chambers, *The Workshop of the World* (1961), pp. 207–10.

[2] Most of the material in this essay is drawn from my own study of the New Poor Law in the West Riding of Yorkshire, based on the volumes of correspondence between the Boards of Guardians in the West Riding and the Poor Law Commission and Poor Law Board now deposited in the Public Record Office with the Ministry of Health papers (Category MH. 12), and on the local records of overseers and Boards of Guardians, where these exist.

M. E. Rose, '*Poor Law Administration in the West Riding of Yorkshire 1820–1855*', (D.Phil. Oxon, 1965).

Mr Rhodes Boyson has carried out a similar study of seven Unions in North East Lancashire. R. Boyson, 'The New Poor Law in North East Lancashire 1834–1871', *Transactions of the Lancashire and Cheshire Antiquarian Society*, Vol. lxx (1960), pp. 35–56; Ibid. '*Poor Law Administration in North East Lancashire, 1834–1871*' (M.A. Manchester, 1960).

The introduction and working of the New Poor Law in Manchester has been described by the late Professor Redford.

A. Redford, *History of Local Government in Manchester, Vol. ii, Borough and City* (1940), Chapter XVIII.

complacency by the West Riding press. 'The ministerial plan for the improvement of the Poor Laws will excite the general appro-bation of the empire', proclaimed the *Leeds Times* which was later to become a pronounced opponent of the measure.[1] The *Sheffield Independent* decried the attempts of a section of the national press, led by the *Times*, to mislead the public over the Bill, whilst the *Independent*'s Tory rival, the *Mercury*, criticized the Bill only because it was not stringent enough.[2] Such favourable comment, however, was coloured by a 'holier than thou' attitude towards poor law administrators in the rural parishes of southern England. They had failed to reform their administration and, therefore, must have reform thrust upon them. The industrial townships of the West Riding on the other hand, had saved themselves by their own exertions, and thus the New Poor Law was neither designed for, nor required in, the area. 'It is not, however, for the North that this Bill is required', a Sheffield M.P. assured his constituents through the columns of the *Independent*.[3] The *Leeds Mercury* thought that it could 'scarcely be doubted that the Commission will direct interference chiefly on parishes where great abuses exist and not trouble with vexatious meddling the parishes where the affairs of the poor are well administered'.[4]

Many of the industrial townships in the West Riding and in Lancashire considered themselves to be 'well administered' as far as the poor law was concerned, and thus to be above vexatious meddling. The social problems which the industrialization of the late eighteenth and early nineteenth century had created drove them to reform. The upsurge of population, the increase in the number of applicants for poor relief, especially in a period of trade depression, the influx of migrants with settlements in some other parish, the erection of new factories, warehouses, shops and houses, all of which had to be assessed for poor rate purposes, proved too much for the unpaid, part time parish overseer and the unwieldy, infrequent parish vestry meetings to cope with. Thus townships began to elect small committees with the specific task of supervising poor law administration, and to appoint salaried

[1] *Leeds Times*, April 26, 1834. Although the paper later attacked the clauses in the Act which introduced a system of plural voting for the election of Guardians.
  Leeds Times, June 14, 1834.
[2] *Sheffield Independent*, May 10, 1834.
  Sheffield Mercury, April 26, 1834.
[3] *Sheffield Independent*, May 31, 1834.
[4] *Leeds Mercury*, May 31, 1834.

officers to carry out the day-to-day tasks involved in the relief of the poor. In Leeds, poor law matters were controlled by a work-house board of churchwardens, overseers and elected trustees, who styled themselves 'guardians of the poor'.[1] Manchester by 1808 was employing ten standing overseers, 61 district overseers, seven assessors of factories and seven rate collectors, as well as a workhouse governor with a salary of £140 a year.[2] Smaller town-ships like Bingley, Wike and Liversedge, also had supervisory relief committees by 1805 or earlier.[3]

Reforming activity of this nature was given further impetus by Sturges Bourne's Act of 1819 which provided statutory powers for the appointment of select vestries to supervise poor law administration and of salaried assistant overseers to carry out their instructions.[4] Even more important as a stimulus to reform was the trade depression of the immediate post-war years, which sent up relief costs in the West Riding from £258,000 in 1815 to £347,000 in 1820, and in Lancashire from £213,000 in 1815 to £373,000 in 1818, and which led to public meetings of alarmed ratepayers and committees of enquiry into the causes of the increased poor rates in some townships.[5] Reform of local poor law administration along the lines suggested by Sturges Bourne's Act followed in many cases. By 1830, about half of Lancashire's townships had select vestries and assistant overseers, and about a quarter of the West Riding's.[6] The select vestries, consisting of between five and twenty elected members, usually local manu-facturers or tradesmen, together with the vicar, churchwardens and overseers of the parish as ex-officio members, differed little in function or composition from the Boards of Guardians estab-lished after the Act of 1834. Likewise the assistant overseers who inquired into the circumstances of relief applicants and relieved them according to the directions of the select vestry, resembled the relieving officers of the New Poor Law.

[1] Leeds Workhouse Committee. Minute and Order Book, 1818–1824. Leeds City Library Archives, LO M/6.

[2] A. Redford, *History of Local Government in Manchester*, Vol. ii (1940), p. 103.

[3] Overseers' Book, Wike (1787), Bradford Public Library; E. E. Dodd, *Bingley Parish and Township Records* (1953), chapter III; Rev. H. Roberson, *The Select Vestry, or Parish Committee* (1818), p. 40.

[4] 59. Geo. III. c. 12.

[5] Parl. Papers, 1830–31 (52) XI; Sheffield City Library, *Local Pamphlets*, Vol. 102, No. 10, Wentworth Woodhouse Muniments, H. 172.

[6] Parl. Papers, 1830–31 (219) XI. Lancashire had 231 townships with assistant overseers and 202 with select vestries. The West Riding had 160 with assistant overseers and 161 with select vestries.

Administrative reform resulted in some cases in a stricter policy with regard to relief. After its appointment in 1820 Dewsbury's select vestry carried out a detailed enquiry into the condition of those in receipt of poor relief. In 1828, it resolved that the weekly relief list be scrutinized, and as many names as possible removed from it.[1] Liverpool's select vestry resolved at one of its first meetings in 1821 that no relief in money be given to those able to work.[2] In Sheffield, in the same year, the scale of relief to able-bodied paupers was cut drastically, whilst the practice of paying rents for paupers and of making up wages out of the poor rates seems to have been stopped at about the same time.[3]

Able-bodied men who applied for relief were often ordered to perform some task of work such as street sweeping as a condition of their receiving relief. Even the use of the 'well regulated workhouse' was not unknown to northern administrators of the old poor law system. A Liverpool overseer proudly told a Select Committee in 1828 that the numbers on outdoor relief in the town had fallen since the select vestry established a well disciplined workhouse.[4] A Bingley magistrate argued that the 'workhouse system' had been used in the township for twenty years before the Poor Law Amendment Act was passed, whilst even one of the most doctrinaire of the Poor Law Commission's assistants after 1834 found Sheffield's workhouse to be 'capital' when he visited it in 1837.[5]

Despite this, however, the workhouse was mainly used as a threat to deter those who were thought to be idle and dissolute, especially Irish vagrants, from applying to the parish for relief, and to force some of those who were granted outdoor relief to accept a smaller weekly sum, if they wished to avoid being sent to the workhouse.[6] As will be seen, relief in the workhouse, indoor relief, was, and was to remain, an exceptional device for the poor law administrator in an industrial area to use.

By the early 1830s it seemed to poor law administrators in

---

[1] Dewsbury Select Vestry. Minute Book. April 17, 1820. October 13, 1828. Dewsbury Public Library.

[2] S.C. Employment or Relief of Able Bodied from the Poors' Rate, 1828 (494) IV. Evidence of Lister Ellis, p. 53.

[3] R.C. Poor Laws (1834), Appendix A, Part 1, No. 20, p. 852.

[4] S.C. 1828 (494) IV. Evidence of Lister Ellis, p. 54.

[5] W. Ellis to P.L.C., Dec. 31, 1836. P.R.O. MH 12/15158; E. Gulson to P.L.C., May 16, 1837. P.R.O. MH 12/15465.

[6] R.C. Poor Laws (1834), App. A, Part I, No. 20, pp. 808, 842; Leeds Workhouse Committee, Minute and Order Book, Jan. 28, 1818.

those townships where reform had been carried out that their efforts had been greeted with success. As proof of this, they had only to point to the statistics of relief expenditure. In 1831, poor relief in Lancashire cost 4s. 4d. per head of the county's population, and, in the West Riding, 5s. 7d. By contrast Suffolk spent 18s. 3d. per head of its population in relieving paupers, Wiltshire 16s. 6d., and Norfolk 15s. 4d.[1] Thus, in 1834, the industrial townships of Lancashire and the West Riding gloried in their competent administration, and left the New Poor Law to the pauperized Southern counties, for which it was intended. A further fall in relief expenditure during the prosperous years of 1835 and 1836 only served to confirm them in this opinion. They failed to take account of the fact that high labour demand in their townships placed them in a favourable position with regard to poor relief, whatever the state of their administration. Thus they were enraged when the Poor Law Commission sent Assistant Commissioners northwards in 1837 to break up the administration of the townships and form Poor Law Unions administered by Boards of Guardians under the control of the central authority. 'The general feeling is this,' a select vestryman from Gomersal told a Select Committee in 1838, "what a pity that a system which has worked so well and has produced so much good should be broken up!" That is the universal exclamation. I am not speaking of the working classes for they do not understand these things: but amongst the most respectable portion of the ratepayers, the clergymen and such gentry as we have, and the principal ratepayers, that is the universal feeling.'[2] This feeling of pride in their administration, and hostility to a central authority who wished to interfere with it, was one of the most powerful obstacles to the success of the New Poor Law in the industrial areas of Lancashire and the West Riding.

The Poor Law Commission, which had been set up by the Act of 1834 to organize the country into Poor Law Unions and to control relief policy within them, was surprised by the hostility which met its attempt to do this in the North of England in 1837. Like the local authorities who opposed it, it believed the North to be well administered as far as the poor law was concerned. From this belief, however, it drew entirely opposite conclusions from

[1] A. Ure, *Philosophy of Manufactures* (1835), p. 477.
[2] S.C. Poor Law Amendment Act, 1837–8, XVIII, Q. 5293.

those of the township administrators. Instead of holding that the New Poor Law was not required in the North, it believed that the new system would be easy to introduce there since it differed so little from the old one. Thus, the Commissioners ignored the advice of their Secretary, that obstinate Mancunian, Edwin Chadwick, who urged them to begin their work in the North in 1835 whilst the winds of trade stood fair.[1] They began to organize the new Unions in the southern counties which seemed to need them most, and only turned northwards in 1837. Obsessed as they were with the problems of agrarian pauperism, they had given no thought to the special problems of the industrial areas, problems such as those caused by cyclical or structural unemployment or by labour migration.

When the Poor Law Commission finally turned their attention northwards in 1837, the industrial townships were in no mood to receive them. The onset of trade depression in that year aroused the fears of the working classes lest, under the New Poor Law system, they be denied a dole from the poor rates to tide them over a period of unemployment and short time working, and be sent with their families to a grim workhouse, a New Poor Law 'Bastile'. The New Poor Law seemed to them but another episode in the campaign waged against the working classes by the Whig Government, a campaign which had brought their exclusion from the terms of the Reform Act of 1832, the defeat of the Ten Hours Bill in 1833, and the attacks against trade unions in 1833 and 1834. Not only were they in no mood to receive the New Poor Law in 1837, they were extremely well organized, through the medium of the Ten Hours Movement, to resist it. The Short Time Committees of Lancashire and the West Riding turned from the factory reform campaign, to march, under the same leaders, against the New Poor Law.

The story of the Anti Poor Law Movement has been chronicled too often to require retelling here.[2] From platform and press, its leaders attacked the inhumanity and irreligion of the new system of relief. They told dreadful tales of New Poor Law cruelties which were at best half truths, and which at worst would stand comparison with the Gothic horror stories of Mrs Radcliffe and

[1] Finer, op. cit., p. 115.
[2] Vide, for example, the accounts in: M. Hovell, *The Chartist Movement* (2nd Ed., 1925); C. Driver, *Tory Radical. The Life of Richard Oastler* (1946); J. T. Ward, *The Factory Movement, 1830–1855* (1962).

Mary Shelley.[1] These methods were successful, however, in rousing the working classes to such a pitch of fury that the introduction of the New Poor Law was greeted in some places by an outburst of mob violence. Troops had to be called upon to check rioting, and an alarmed Home Secretary urged the Poor Law Commission to proceed with extreme caution in their task of introducing the New Poor Law in the disturbed areas.[2]

Inhumanity was not the only feature of the New Poor Law which the leaders of the Anti Poor Law Movement condemned. Many of them were equally incensed at the attempts of a newly formed central authority, the 'Three Bashaws of Somerset House', to interfere with a long established system of local administration. The leading Anti Poor Law agitators had good reason to be affectionate towards the old system of poor law administration. John Fielden and W. B. Ferrand were local J.P.s, and as such were charged with the oversight of the parochial system of poor law administration in their districts. Samuel Roberts, the ageing Sheffield silver plater and philanthropist, who was amongst the leading pamphleteers of the Movement, had served as an overseer in Sheffield. Richard Oastler's father, Robert, had been a prominent member of the Leeds workhouse committee. They wished to preserve the old order of society, and thus they opposed anything which threatened to disrupt that order, whether it be factories, universal suffrage or Government centralization. Oastler, in a speech at Halifax, remarked that, even if the New Poor Law should be found to make paupers happier, 'he would oppose it still, because it interfered with every local right, and because it attacked every man in every corner of the land'.[3] 'If, Sir, you really do wish to benefit us, only be so good as to desire your employers to request their employers to LET US ALONE', wrote Samuel Roberts in an open letter to Edwin Chadwick.[4]

This cry of 'let us alone' was the most formidable which the Poor Law Commission had to face in the North. Formidable because it was supported by many local magistrates and poor law administrators who did not wish to have their authority weakened by an interfering Commission. Even those who disliked the

[1] For a selection of these, vide: G. R. Wythen Baxter, *The Book of Bastilles* (1841).
[2] Home Secretary to P.L.C., June 27, 1837. P.R.O. MH 12/15063.
[3] Quoted in Baxter G.R.W., *The Book of Bastilles* (1841), p. 400.
[4] S. Roberts, *Letter to Edwin Chadwick Esq., on His Coming to Sheffield* (1843). Sheffield City Library. *Local Pamphlets*, Vol. 13, No. 2.

personalities and methods of the Anti Poor Law Movement were often equally distrustful of the New Poor Law system. William Ellis, a Bingley magistrate, complained bitterly about the activities of his neighbour, Busfield Ferrand, but, in 1836, he wrote to the Poor Law Commission, pleading the case for the exclusion of Bingley from a New Poor Law Union, and, even in 1842, was still convinced that 'the New Poor Law was not called for or required in the Keighley Union'.[1]

Those who held such opinions soon found a more effective method of resisting the central authority than through the semi-violent protests of the Anti Poor Law Movement which might involve rioting and the destruction of property. It had at first been feared that the new local authority for poor law purposes, the Boards of Guardians, would be mere puppets of the central authority, 'the tools of the Commission as the cutler's hammer was his', a speaker told a Sheffield Anti Poor Law meeting.[2] This fear, however, proved groundless. Alarmed by the North's violent reaction to the New Poor Law, the Poor Law Commission were forced to tread warily, introducing the new system by degrees and allowing the widest powers of discretion to the new Boards of Guardians in order to win their confidence. The new Boards, with local J.P.s as ex-officio members and many former township poor law administrators amongst their elected membership, were determined to resist the Poor Law Commission to the extent of breaking the new system or at least of bending it as close to the old system as possible. Hostility to central control, that most powerful weapon in the armoury of the Anti Poor Law Movement, was lodged after 1837 in many of the Board rooms of Lancashire and the West Riding for use against any unwarranted interference by Poor Law Commission or Poor Law Board. 'The rabble are easily quieted', wrote one Assistant Poor Law Commissioner in 1838, 'but where a majority of a Board of Guardians is opposed to the Commissioners, the whole proceedings are attended with extreme difficulty.'[3]

The proceeding which the central authority found to be attended with most difficulty was that of trying to make Boards of Guardians in the industrial areas alter their system of giving relief

[1] Wm. Ellis to P.L.C., Dec. 31, 1836. Ibid. to A. Power, Sept. 8, 1840. Ibid. to W. Clapham, Feb. 9, 1842. P.R.O. MH 12/15158.
[2] *Sheffield Iris*, May 9, 1837. Reporting speech by Rev. W. Hill.
[3] Charles Mott to P. L. Comm., Aug. 16, 1838. P.R.O. MH 12/14830.

in order to conform to the principles laid down in the 1834 Report. In the order which they issued to Boards of Guardians in Lancashire and the West Riding in 1838, the Poor Law Commission merely asked the Guardians to assume control of relief administration in the townships of their Union, 'at such times, respectively, and in such order as they shall deem fitting and convenient'. Once they had taken control, the Guardians were to continue to administer relief under the terms of the Act of 1601.[1] This order contrasted sharply with the first order issued to the Boards of Guardians in the southern counties in 1835, which contained detailed regulations as to the administration of relief, particularly with regard to the able-bodied poor.[2] Thus, in the early years of their existence, Boards of Guardians in the northern industrial areas were given wide powers of discretion in the mode of administering poor relief. This was a position they were unwilling to surrender in later years.

In general, these discretionary powers were used by the Guardians to continue the relief system established by their predecessors in the townships. The basis of the system was the granting of small doles, usually in cash, to applicants for relief. Few scales of relief were drawn up, but in general, grants were made on the basis of 1s. 0d. or 1s. 6d. a week for each member of a family, with an increase to 2s. 0d. or 2s. 6d. for an old person. Most authorities realised that this was barely sufficient for maintenance, but argued that applicants usually had other sources of income to supplement their relief. In periods of trade depression, when able-bodied applicants for relief were most numerous, funds were raised by voluntary effort in the industrial towns to supply the poor with soup, potatoes, blankets, fuel and occasionally, cash. For the aged, gifts from permanent charities, or the meagre earnings from some simple task of work such as selling matches or newspapers, could be used to eke out the few shillings granted in poor relief. Handicraft workers, such as worsted or cotton hand loom weavers or woolcombers who had fallen on bad times, might still earn a little at their trade to add to their poor relief, in addition to the earnings which their wives or children might be able to bring home. At Sheffield, in 1820, there were loud complaints about cutlery workers drawing parish relief and continuing

[1] P.L.C. 4th Annual Report (1838), Appendix A, No. 7.
[2] P.L.C. 1st Ann. Report (1835), App. A, No. 6.

to produce goods at ruinously low prices, thus overstocking an already depressed market.[1] Although the practice seems to have been checked in Sheffield in the 1820s, it continued elsewhere, especially in parishes where handloom weavers' earnings were being driven down by machine competition, so that those with large families were unable to maintain them without aid from the rates. Practically all outdoor relief was relief in aid of something, whether it be earnings or grants from private charities.

To parochial administrators and later to the Boards of Guardians in the industrial areas, outdoor relief of this type seemed the cheapest and most convenient policy. Most townships had their own workhouse, or shared one with other townships, but these were generally reserved for the care of those unable to care for themselves if given outdoor relief, old people, invalids or mental defectives with no relatives to look after them, and orphan or deserted children.

At the discretion of the overseers or the select vestry, able-bodied paupers might be threatened with relief in the workhouse if they were thought to be idlers, but usually the threat was enough, and the proportion of able-bodied paupers in the workhouses of Lancashire and the West Riding was a tiny one. Obviously, no workhouse was large enough to contain all those who applied for relief in a year like 1826 or 1842, but even in prosperous years, when few able-bodied poor applied for relief, local administrators were generally hesitant in granting relief in the workhouse. Indoor relief was more expensive than outdoor. In 1854, it was estimated that in Lancashire and the West Riding, indoor paupers each cost £5. 10s. 0d. a year to maintain, as compared to £3. 11s. 0d. for an outdoor pauper.[2] If an underemployed hand-loom weaver and his family were ordered into the workhouse, the parish would become responsible for the whole cost of their relief, with no immediate prospect of their leaving the workhouse. If outdoor relief were given, however, a small dole might suffice which, added to the weaver's meagre earnings, would tide the family over a lean period until, with the return of better times, their earnings might be sufficient to maintain them unaided.

The same argument applied to the old and sick. At Gomersal, the select vestry preferred to keep aged paupers at home, where

[1] Sheffield City Library. *Local Pamphlets*, Vol. 102, No. 10.
[2] S.C. Removal of Paupers, 1854–5, XIII, Q. 3033.

they were said to be more comfortable and could be kept for 2s. 6d. a week, whereas in the workhouse they would have cost 3s. 6d.[1] Motives of humanity were blended none too subtly with those of economy.

A similar mixture of motives led Boards of Guardians in the industrial areas after 1837 to continue this policy of relief, and to oppose any attempts by the central authority to tamper with it. Many Boards of Guardians opposed the attempts of the central authority to persuade them to build a new Union workhouse, because such a building seemed a symbol of the hated new system and might be used to introduce a policy of prohibiting outdoor relief to the able bodied. 'We have not a workhouse; we have a poorhouse; and I hope we shall never live to see a work-house at Keighley', pronounced a member of that Board of Guardians in 1842.[2] But another factor hindering the provision of new workhouses was the capital cost of their erection and the prospect of saddling the Union with the heavy burden of debt repayments. Although by 1854, 16 of the 27 West Riding Unions had agreed to erect a new workhouse, no Poor Law institutions, with the exception of the Leeds Industrial School, were built during the 1840s, a decade whose opening and closing years were ones of severe pressure on the poor rates of Unions in the industrial areas.[3] Twenty years after the extension of the New Poor Law to the area, several Unions were still making use of the old inadequate township poorhouses for the purpose of indoor relief.

No system of compulsory indoor relief was clamped on the industrial areas of Lancashire and the West Riding. In the early 1840s, only about 8 per cent of those relieved in the West Riding were in the workhouse, as compared to about 15 per cent in the country as a whole.[4] In 1855, able-bodied paupers in West Riding workhouses were only about 4 per cent of all able-bodied relieved, whilst the national average was about 14 per cent.[5] As early as October 1837, the Poor Law Commission were advised by one of their Assistants in the industrial districts of Lancashire

[1] S.C. Poor Law Amendment Act, 1837–8, XVIII, Q. 5355, 5443–4.
[2] S.C. Keighley Union, 1842, IX, Q. 731.
[3] P.L.C. 5th Ann. Report (1839), App. D, No. 4, Part III; P.L.B. 2nd–8th Ann. Reports (1849–55); Leeds Intelligencer, Oct. 17, 1846.
[4] J. R. McCulloch, A Descriptive and Statistical Account of the British Empire (1847 Ed.), Vol. ii, pp. 664, 670.
[5] P.L.B. 8th Ann. Report (1855), App. No. 36.

and the West Riding as to the unsuitability of any 'workhouse test' system for these areas.[1] The Commission heeded this advice and did not impose their Outdoor Relief Prohibitory Order on any of the industrial Unions in the area.

Despite their concessions in this matter, however, the Poor Law Commission were anxious to exercise some control over the relief policy of Boards of Guardians in the industrial areas, and in particular to check such practices as relief in aid of earnings. In this determination they frequently clashed with the Guardians who did not wish to see the established relief system, which was both cheap and convenient, undermined.

In the early 1840s, the Poor Law Commission began to issue an Outdoor Labour Test Order to Boards of Guardians in the industrial areas. Under the terms of this, able-bodied male applicants for relief were to be set to do a task of work by the Guardians as a condition of receiving outdoor relief, half of which was to be given in kind. Relief to those in employment and the payment of rents out of poor relief funds were forbidden.[2]

Boards of Guardians did not take kindly to this interference with their powers of discretion. They complained that a labour test was costly to operate, that hard physical labour was unsuitable for those who normally pursued sedentary occupations like woolcombing or weaving, that it was degrading for those unemployed through no fault of their own to be set to work with idle and dissolute paupers, and that prohibition of rent payments would lead to the eviction from their homes and workshops of many handicraft workers, a proceeding which, Bradford Guardians maintained, 'would drive them to despair and recklessly and literally destroy their moral independence.'[3]

Despite their protests, however, Boards of Guardians did not find their powers too greatly restricted by the Labour Test Order. It applied only to able-bodied males, and even here exemption could be granted in cases of sickness and 'sudden and urgent necessity', and also in other cases provided these were reported to the central authority within fifteen days of relief being given. Halifax Guardians continually used this device to delay the introduction of a labour test in the winter of 1843–4, the Poor

[1] A. Power to P.L.C., Oct. 21, 1837. P.R.O. MH 32/63.
[2] P.L.C. 8th Ann. Report (1842), App. A, No. 11.
[3] Memorial to P.L.C. from Bradford Board of Guardians, June 7, 1843. P.R.O. MH 12/14723.

Law Commission reluctantly accepting their excuses for evading the Order.[1]

The Poor Law Commission's chief weapon against such evasions was the threat of financial sanctions. Relief payments made in contravention of the Order might be disallowed by the auditor and surcharged to the Guardians' own pockets. This weapon was strengthened in 1844 when Union auditors were replaced by district auditors who scrutinized the accounts of a number of Unions and were less subject to pressure from any particular Board of Guardians.[2] Even so, the Poor Law Commission had to use this weapon with extreme care. An auditor who was too strict was likely to cause a revolt. Huddersfield Guardians, faced with an unsympathetic auditor in 1846, threatened to resign in a body if they were to be forced to carry out the orders of the Commission 'in their literal and grammatical sense'.[3]

The Poor Law Board, which succeeded the Poor Law Commission in 1847, attempted to obtain firmer control of the relief policy of Boards of Guardians than their feeble predecessors had done. In August 1852, they issued an Outdoor Relief Regulation Order to Boards of Guardians in Lancashire, the West Riding and the London area. This Order repeated the provisions of the Labour Test Order, and also laid down that a portion of the outdoor relief granted to non able-bodied paupers was to be in kind.[4] A storm of protest greeted this attempt to widen the scope of central interference with the Guardians' powers of giving relief. Boards of Guardians in Lancashire and the West Riding bombarded the Poor Law Board with petitions and letters of protest, and a meeting of representatives from Northern Boards of Guardians met in Manchester to organize a collective protest against the Order.[5]

In face of this attack by the Boards of Guardians, the Poor Law Board was forced to issue a new modified Order in December 1852.[6] This omitted all mention of relief to non able-bodied

---

[1] Correspondence between Halifax Board of Guardians and P.L.C., Jan.–July 1844. P.R.O. MH 12/14976.

[2] 7 and 8 Vic., c. 101, ss. 32–37.

[3] Huddersfield Board of Guardians to P.L.C., Aug. 1846. P.R.O. MH 12/15068. The Board's chairman, the Reverend J. M. Maxfield, also made a public protest. Vide: his letter in *The Times*, Sept. 5, 1846.

[4] P.L.B. 5th Ann. Report (1852), App. No. 1.

[5] *Leeds Times*, Oct. 30, 1852; *Sheffield Independent*, Oct. 30, 1852; a number of the resolutions of protest from individual Unions are printed in Parl. Papers, 1852–3 (111) LXXXIV.

[6] P.L.B. 5th Ann. Report (1852), App. No. 3.

paupers, and, although it still prohibited relief in aid of earnings, the Instructional Letter accompanying it weakened this prohibition considerably. It was to apply only to 'the giving of relief at the same identical time as that at which the person receiving it is in actual employment and in the receipt of wages', and not to 'a man working for wages on one day and being without work the next, or working half the week, and being unemployed the remainder.'[1] Under such conditions, evasion was easy. Outdoor relief in aid of wages and earnings continued as under the old system, and may well have enabled some handicraft workers to maintain their hopeless struggle against the machine for longer than would otherwise have been possible. Resistance to central authority resulted in its failure to control the poor relief system as the 1834 reformers had intended.

The survival of the old system of relief in the industrial Unions of Lancashire and the West Riding should not be seen too much in terms of a victory for practical humanity over doctrinaire bureaucrats who wished to impose the 1834 workhouse system. As has been seen, the Poor Law Commission was willing to compromise over the question of the 'workhouse test', which was quite unsuitable for the industrial areas. All they wished to do was to eliminate some of the abuses which they believed had crept into the system of relief in the North. Their attempts to do so were fought at every turn by the local administrators who claimed the old system was more humane than any which could be devised by the central authority. There was little that was humane, however, in a system which gave a meagre dole to the unfortunate, and then left them to make out as best they might, or which sent the helpless to badly administered, overcrowded and insanitary township poorhouses.[2] The old poor law system could be very cruel especially to vagrants, parish apprentices or unmarried mothers. Inhumanity was by no means the new found prerogative of Edwin Chadwick and the 'Three Bashaws of Somerset House'.

The demand for discretionary powers on the part of Boards of Guardians in the northern industrial areas was often prompted as

---

[1] P.L.B. 5th Ann. Report, App. No. 4.
[2] The West Riding's equivalent of the 'Andover scandal' in the 1840s, occurred, not in a New Poor Law 'Bastille', but in the Huddersfield township poorhouse when it was hit by a typhus epidemic in 1848; A. Austin to P.L.B., July 11, 1848, and newspaper cuttings enclosed in correspondence of Huddersfield Board of Guardians and P.L.B. May–June 1848. P.R.O. MH 12/15070.

much by a desire for economy as for humanity. The retention of the system of giving small doles to supplement other earnings and the opposition to expensive workhouse building schemes were prompted by the need to save the rates. Thus, the Guardians have been condemned as men of little imagination or foresight, whose whole administrative effort was directed to keeping down the poor rate in the interests of the petty bourgeois class, farmers, shopkeepers and small manufacturers, from which they were largely drawn. The writings of Dickens and the cartoons of *Punch* portrayed them as corrupt, fat and self interested, caring little for the poor and much for the rates. A recent historian, discussing the role of shopkeepers on Boards of Guardians, has remarked, 'the impression they leave is not always pleasant, for they could be very anxious to avoid expenditure, rather self assured, and very hard on the poor'.[1] Such a verdict could fairly be applied to many members of Boards of Guardians, both in the northern industrial areas and elsewhere, although it should be remembered that some of their colleagues were humane men with progressive ideas, and many more were conscientious men who attended faithfully to the depressing task of relieving the poor.

Nor was the desire for economy altogether selfish or misplaced in view of the failure of the Act of 1834 to make any substantial reform in the financial basis of the poor law system. In the matter of assessing and collecting the poor rate, the parish, and not the Union, remained the body responsible after 1834. The Guardians decided matters of relief policy, but were dependent on the overseers for the financing of their decisions. Until 1865, each parish was separately responsible for the cost of relieving paupers belonging to it.[2] The cost of such items as the building or improvement of a Union workhouse, or the salaries of Union officers, was met from a common fund to which each member parish contributed according to an assessment laid on it. Until 1861, this assessment was based not on the rateable value of a parish but on its average annual relief expenditure, on its poverty rather than on its property.[3]

---

[1] G. Kitson Clark, *The Making of Victorian England* (1961), p. 122.

[2] 4 & 5 Wm. IV, c. 76, s. 26. This was amended by the Union Chargeability Act (1865) (28 & 29 Vic., c. 79), under which the whole cost of poor relief was charged to the common fund of the Union.

[3] 4 & 5 Wm. IV, c. 76, s. 28. This was amended by the 24 & 25 Vic., c. 55, s. 9, under which rateable value not relief expenditure was made the basis of assessment.

Such a system inevitably created friction between parishes with a large amount of cottage property, a low rateable value and a high relief expenditure, and those with wealthy residents, few paupers and property of a high rateable value. In Knaresborough Union, for example, Knaresborough township was assessed to the common fund on the basis of an annual relief expenditure of £1,500, whilst nearby Harrogate was assessed at only £400.[1] Although its rateable value was £5,000 more than Knaresborough's, the fashionable watering place did little or nothing towards aiding its fellow parish in the Union, despite the fact that Knaresborough's ratepayers were weighed down with the cost of relieving local linen weavers who had fallen on hard times.

As well as creating bad feeling between wealthy and poor parishes, the common fund system also led to tension between rural and urban parishes in the same Union. Many of the Unions in Lancashire and the West Riding were centred on industrial towns like Bradford or Halifax but included within their boundaries a large number of small rural townships, each of which elected a representative to the Board of Guardians. Such townships objected to contributing to a common fund which would be used to enlarge a workhouse or pay an officer mainly for the benefit of the larger number of paupers relieved in the industrial town. These townships, therefore, returned Guardians to the Board whose main object was to oppose any proposals which might increase the burden of the common fund. The little township of Clifton in the Halifax Union elected a Guardian in 1847 for the express purpose of opposing a plan to build a new fever hospital in the Union.[2] In Bradford, the rural Guardians refused to agree to improvements at the workhouse unless they were carried out at the expense of Bradford township alone.[3] Guardians from the rural townships were able to command a majority on several Boards, and thus defeat any of the proposals of the town Guardians. Progressive Guardians were hindered by the actions of their fellows who continued to put the interests of their parishes before that of the Union. Significantly, the most far sighted measures approved by the Boards of Guardians in the area after 1837, the building of Industrial Schools at Leeds and Manchester

[1] P.L.B. 7th Ann. Report (1854), App. 37.
[2] Halifax Board of Guardians to P.L.C., June 10, 1847. P.R.O. MH 12/14977.
[3] Bradford Board of Guardians to P.L.C., Dec. 20, 1838. P.R.O. MH 12/14720.

and the Hollow Meadows farm scheme for able-bodied male paupers at Sheffield, were carried out in Unions which had no extensive rural hinterland.[1]

Even where the reluctance of the rural Guardians to spend money could be overcome, progress was hampered by the precarious financial basis on which Boards of Guardians in the industrial areas had to work. The building of factories and other commercial premises, of railways and canals in and around the industrial towns during this period had certainly added to their rateable value. Stock in trade, however, was found not to be liable to assessment for poor rate purposes, and overseers found considerable difficulty in assessing railways, canals and coal mines in their townships.[2] A considerable proportion of the poor rate still had to be borne by occupiers of house property, and, in many cases, by occupiers of quite humble means. Leeds, in 1847, contained 23,000 rateable houses and other premises, 17,000 of which were rated at under £10 a year.[3] In 1851, one-third of the poor rate assessments in Sheffield and Barnsley, half of those in Halifax and Wakefield, and two-thirds of those in Dewsbury were made on property with a rateable value of less than £4 a year.[4]

Collection of the rate from such premises proved difficult, especially in periods of trade depression. The occupiers often moved house without warning, leaving the property empty or occupied by new tenants whose names did not appear in the rate books and who could not, therefore, be held responsible for the amount owed. Even those who remained in their houses might be unable due to poverty to pay their rates, and, if taken to court, were usually excused payment by the magistrates. At Dewsbury, in December 1841, 28 per cent of the rate levied was excused or in arrears.[5] Leeds experienced 'leakages' of the poor rate amounting to nearly 20 per cent in lean years like 1842 or 1848.[6]

---

[1] On the Industrial Schools: Vide: Leeds Board of Guardians—Minute Books 1845–1853 passim; A. Redford, *History of Local Government in Manchester*, Vol. ii, p. 127. On Hollow Meadows: Vide: J. Salt, 'Isaac Ironside and the Hollow Meadows Farm Experiment', *Yorks. Bulletin of Economic and Social Research*, Vol. xii, March 1960, pp. 45–51.

[2] E. Cannan, *The History of Local Rates in England* (2nd Ed., 1927), p. 100; S.C. House of Lords on Parochial Assessments (1850) XVI.

[3] S.C. Settlement (1847) XI, Q. 4253.

[4] Returns of Property Assessed to Poor Rates (1851). P.R.O. MH 12/15471, 14765, 15571, 14980, 14834.

[5] Dewsbury Township Rate Book, Dec. 1841. Dewsbury Public Library.

[6] *Leeds Intelligencer*, April 27, 1850.

At such times, parish overseers found great difficulty in meeting calls for funds by the Boards of Guardians. The Guardians, in their turn, found their financial reserves draining away at a time when demands on them were greatest. Huddersfield Guardians owed £2,000 to their bankers in 1841.[1] Wakefield Guardians in 1849 had only £40 to their credit, and needed £240 to meet the weekly relief bill.[2] In such circumstances, the reluctance of Guardians to consent to expensive new projects becomes more understandable. At times when the sources of finance were likely to dry up, every penny had to be kept to meet ordinary weekly expenditure.[3]

In this difficult matter of Union finance, the legislature and the central authority proved singularly unhelpful. The 1834 Report virtually ignored the rating problem.[4] The Poor Law Amendment Act did little to amend poor law finance.[5] Not until 1846 was any grant made available from the Exchequer to relieve the burden borne by the local poor rate.[6] Not until 1850 was legislation passed allowing owners of small cottage property rated at under £6 a year to compound for the rates levied on their property.[7] Only in the 1860s, when the Lancashire Cotton Famine revealed to the full the weaknesses of the rating system in the industrial areas were any radical changes made, and even then considerable. anomalies and inequalities, particularly between Union and Union, remained.[8]

[1] Huddersfield Board of Guardians—Minute Book, March 12, 1841.
[2] *Leeds Mercury*, April 7, 1849.
[3] Other local government bodies faced similar difficulties in the 19th century. Vide: E. P. Hennock, 'Finance and Politics in Urban Local Government, 1835–1900', *Historical Journal*, Vol. vi (1963), pp. 212–25.
[4] It condemned the existing mode of rating as 'uncertain and capricious', but having rejected the idea of making the cost of poor relief a national charge, it made no detailed recommendations regarding the reform of the poor rate. R.C. Poor Laws (1834). Report (1905 Edition, Cd. 2728), pp. 178–80, 359–60.
[5] Three permissive sections in the Act gave Unions power to declare themselves as one parish for rating purposes, but these seem to have proved abortive. 4 & 5 Wm. IV, c. 76, ss. 34–36.
[6] Grants were made to help pay the salaries of Union medical officers and workhouse teachers. P.L.C. 13th Ann. Report (1847), pp. 25–6 and App. A.
[7] By the Small Tenements Rating Act (13 & 14 Vic., c. 99, s. 1). Sturges Bourne's Act had allowed for the rating of owners, but only with regard to property valued at between £6 and £20 a year. 59 Geo. III, c. 12, s. 19.
[8] 24 & 25 Vic., c. 55, s. 9 (1861) made rateable value not relief expenditure the basis of assessment for the common fund.
25 & 26 Vic., c. 103 (1862) transferred powers of making assessments for rating purposes from parish overseers to Boards of Guardians, and compelled other parishes in a Union to aid those burdened by high poor rates.
28 & 29 Vic., c. 79 (Union Chargeability Act 1865) made the whole cost of poor relief chargeable to the Union instead of to the individual parishes.

The Government and the Poor Law Commission showed a similar lack of understanding of the poor relief problems of the northern industrial areas in the matter of the laws of settlement. The Royal Commission of 1834 took little heed of the difficulties raised by this tangled code of complex legislation. It recommended some reform of the settlement laws, but these recommendations were only partially carried into effect by the Act of 1834, which, if anything, left the situation more complicated than before.[1]

The problems raised by the laws of settlement were particularly great in northern industrial townships which, in the early nineteenth century, were receiving large numbers of immigrants from the surrounding countryside and also from Ireland. Local poor law administrators had, however, overcome some of the difficulties caused by settlement legislation by means of a system of non-resident relief. Under this system, the township in which the applicant for relief was living granted him relief, and was then refunded, at monthly or quarterly intervals, by the township in which the applicant claimed a settlement. Although liable to abuse, the system allowed for the freer movement of the immigrant labour so essential to the developing industries of the northern towns, and prevented the hardship which large numbers of paupers would have suffered had they been removed back to their parishes of settlement in periods of trade depression. Despite its advantages, however, the central authority after 1837 proved singularly unsympathetic to this system of non-resident relief, and made no secret of their dislike, although they were never strong enough to overcome the determination of northern Boards of Guardians to retain this feature of the older poor law code.[2]

This failure to understand the difficulties of coping with the laws of settlement in industrial areas was reflected in the attempt to amend the laws by an Act passed in 1846. Under the terms of this, an unbroken period of residence for five years in a township rendered a person irremovable, and thus the responsibility for poor

[1] The Report urged the simplification of the means of acquiring a settlement, but did not advocate the total repeal of the settlement code since it believed that fear of removal acted as a deterrent to applicants for poor relief. R.C. Poor Laws (1834). Report, op. cit., pp. 152–165, 342–344.

The Poor Law Amendment Act merely prohibited the acquisition of a settlement by hiring and service, serving a parish office, or apprenticeship in the sea service, and even these prohibitions were not made retrospective. 4 & 5 Wm. IV, c. 76, ss. 64, 67.

[2] P.L.C. 9th Ann. Rep. (1843), p. 39.

relief purposes of the township in which he was resident, provided that he had not received poor relief, been in prison, in a lunatic asylum or on military service during the five year qualifying period.[1]

On the face of it, this measure was an act of justice to rural townships who had often had to pay poor relief for paupers who were living in the industrial towns and who, when fully employed, were working to enrich those towns. It was intended as a piece of compensation to the landed classes for the repeal of the Corn Laws.[2] Unfortunately, however, it was so ill thought out and hastily drafted that there was doubt as to whether the proviso governing the qualifying period of residence was retrospective or not. It was held at first that it was not retrospective, and thus a large number of paupers in the industrial towns who had been receiving non-resident relief now acquired a five year residence and thus irremovability.[3] Industrial townships found themselves suddenly saddled with a large increase in their relief expenditure at a time when trade depression and Irish vagrancy were causing anxiety. Thus, whilst townships in rural Unions like Skipton, Thorne or Goole were relieved of between 70 per cent and 80 per cent of their non-resident paupers, over 1,500 persons resident in Leeds but with settlements elsewhere now became a direct charge on the town, adding £3,000 to £4,000 to its annual relief bill.[4] Hostility between rural and urban townships in the industrial Unions was exacerbated, and overseers and Guardians began to resort to desperate schemes for getting rid of non-resident paupers.[5]

The very real possibility of a breakdown of the poor relief system in the industrial areas was only averted by emergency legislation in 1847 which allowed the cost of relieving irremovable paupers to be charged to the common fund of the Union.[6] Further relief came in 1848 when the Court of Queen's Bench ruled that the proviso in the 1846 Act was retrospective and thus

[1] 9 & 10 Vic., c. 66, s. 1.
[2] It was one of those 'shadowy schemes of compensation' which Disraeli treated with uch contempt. B. Disraeli, *Life of Lord George Bentinck* (1852), p. 74.
[3] P.L.C. 13th Ann. Report (1847), p. 31.
[4] Return of Non Resident Paupers Relieved (1847); P.R.O. MH 12/15514, 15552, 14956; S.C. Settlement (1847) XI, Q. 3907–3909, 4077.
[5] Leeds magistrates complained that several townships in the borough were refusing relief to paupers in order to force them to leave the township. *Leeds Intelligencer*, April 10, 1847.
[6] 10 & 11 Vic., c. 110 (1847).

applied to those who had been in receipt of non-resident relief before 1846.[1] Nevertheless, the Act of 1846 cast doubt over the whole future of the laws of settlement. The Act of 1847 was only a temporary measure, renewed annually. Boards of Guardians in the industrial areas were faced with the prospect of a further weakening, or even a total abolition of their powers of removal under the settlement laws. Since this was thought likely to bring an influx of potential paupers, especially Irish paupers, into the Unions, the prospect was no cheerful one.

Their tardiness in reforming the financial basis of the poor law, their failure to understand the advantages of the system of non-resident relief and their bungling revision of the laws of settlement revealed a lack of understanding of the poor relief problems of the northern industrial areas by the Poor Law Commission and the Poor Law Board. Even had they tackled such problems boldly, however, it is doubtful if their solutions would have found acceptance in the townships of Lancashire and the West Riding of Yorkshire. Any radical reform of the laws of settlement or of the system of local rating would almost certainly have led to increased national responsibility for poor relief, to a weakening of the local authorities and a strengthening of the central. This was exactly what local administrators in the northern townships had feared would come to pass if the New Poor Law were imposed on them, and what the Anti Poor Law Movement and the Boards of Guardians had resisted so determinedly and so successfully. Because of their belief in the virtues of their own local system and their hatred of dictation from the centre, they made sure that the New Poor Law in the north differed little from the Old in its methods of relief. Outdoor relief, relief in aid of wages and non-resident relief were still given, the township poorhouses still stood in many Unions. Boards of Guardians demanded, and obtained, wide powers of discretion in the granting of relief. Slowly and painfully, the central authority learned that it must reform not by administrative fiat but by tactful persuasion. By 1878, a Poor Law Inspector remarked, as a matter of course, that 'a very wide discretion must of necessity be left to the local authorities'.[2] Such an idea was a far cry from the Benthamite ideals of Edwin Chadwick.

[1] P.L.B. 1st Ann. Report (1848), p. 12.
[2] S.C. Removal (1878–9) XII, Q. 732.

'You think perhaps that the administration of our Poor Law has been centralized since the law of 1834' wrote John Stuart Mill to a correspondent in 1860. 'Not in the least. The immense abuses that had taken place in the local administration had so terrified the public that the enactment of the law had become possible. But it proved impossible to carry it out. Local authority presently regained its predominance over central authority; and the latter has only managed to retain its nominal powers by exercising them with so excessive a reserve that they have remained rather a reserve for use in extreme cases than a systematic mainspring of administration.'[1] Nowhere was this more true than in the industrial areas of the north of England. 'Localism', intense hostility to centralization, ensured the failure of the New Poor Law. If its birth was hymned by Miss Martineau, its epitaph was spoken by Mr. Podsnap.

'Ah!' said Mr Podsnap. 'Easy to say somewhere; not so easy to say where! But I see what you are driving at. I knew it from the first. Centralization. No. Never with my consent. Not English.'[2]

[1] J. S. Mill to Charles Dupont-White, April 6, 1860. Quoted: Webb, Vol. viii, p. 240.
[2] Charles Dickens, *Our Mutual Friend* (Dickens Fellowship Edition 1906), p. 121.

7

C. M. ELLIOTT

The Political Economy of English Dissent
1780-1840

I

This essay is intended to contribute to the dynamic analysis of the content of Dissenting teaching on some of the social and economic issues, either created or emphasized by the Industrial Revolution. It does not pretend to be either exhaustive or definitive. Local studies provide the richest quarry for this type of analysis: but such studies of a high academic quality are rare. Until social and economic historians exploit more fully the rich veins of local archives, a definitive account of the tensions and evolutions we shall describe must remain unwritten. The apologia for the appearance of this essay is the need for a clearer focus and more sophisticated analytical framework for many of the studies that are in hand. Social and ecclesiastical historians have much of interest and importance to say about the development of a society: their comparative neglect is largely the result, especially in the case of ecclesiastical historians, of the failure to ask sufficiently fundamental questions about the wider implications of the phenomena they describe. If the social sciences are to be reintegrated and therefore rescued from the fissiparous tendency they have shown in the last twenty years, it is important that historians do not allow their specialisms to blind them to the interrelationships manifested by any society, but more particularly one in the process of rapid social change. In the succeeding pages, then, we attempt to show how the phenomena of most interest to the theologian and ecclesiastical historian (largely ignored by others because of their complexity and seeming unreality) reacted upon the whole social complex. This necessarily involves treating the theological changes as independent variables: we do not seek to explain the more fundamental of these changes, such as the emergence of Wesley as a charismatic leader primarily concerned with the lower classes. This is, of course, to distort the picture. Neither theology nor missionary strategy exists separately from the society in which it is taught or conceived. If we believe that social development can be explained, we must concede that there are no independent variables which we are forced to accept as given. Having said that, however, we recognise that any explanation of the past and most worthwhile explanations of the present are circumscribed by the limitations of evidence, which make the assumption of independence somewhere within the system a necessary evil.

Granted, then, the fact of Wesleyan Methodism, with no causal questions asked and none answered, we shall relate the theological changes thus induced to the development of social attitudes and doctrines in the Dissenting Churches. 'The Nonconformist conscience' in the latter half of the nineteenth century has received such adequate notice from historians as to invest it with a misleading substantiality. If the Nonconformist conscience was more subtle and less pervasive than has sometimes been suggested, historians have stressed its importance as one of the poles around which socio-economic thought naturally moved. By the end of the earlier period with which we are concerned, the 'conscience' was less notorious, less sure of its moral bearings, and less monolithic. Previously the Test and Corporation Acts had reduced its public importance, but not its diffuse influence. The Birmingham mob which persecuted Joseph Priestley in 1791 is witness to the importance and influence with which the Dissenters were popularly credited. Yet in the 1790s, this was a relatively new phenomenon. It took Wesley, the American War, the French Revolution and perhaps the intemperate but powerful leadership of Priestley to bring the Dissenters into real contact with the political, social and economic questions of the day.

It is exceedingly difficult to quantify the membership of Dissent. Working backwards, Mann found in 1851 6·8 per cent of the population attended Independent Churches on the day of the Census: 5·2 per cent Baptist Churches and 0·27 per cent Unitarian Churches. The precision of these figures is misleading, but they can be accepted as an indication of the order of magnitude. Halevy thought there were 2,000,000 (c. 20 per cent) Methodists and Dissenters in 1815. Precise regional figures are hard to find. Baines's *Social, Educational and Religious State of the Manufacturing*

Districts: Statistical Returns, is unreliable. A 'corrected' account of the Leeds figures suggests that there the proportion of the whole population of the township of Leeds which was Dissenting or Methodist remained remarkably constant at about one-fifth from 1775 to 1841. This figure again has no pretensions of accuracy and should be taken as a general order of magnitude in a 'typical' expanding manufacturing town rather than as a precise estimate. More or less suspicious as all these figures are, they serve to remind us that the dogmas of a socially-involved Dissent were likely to reach and perhaps influence a significant proportion of the population, especially in the manufacturing towns, where the biggest problems lay.

II

Strictly used, the term Dissenter does not include Wesleyan Methodists, for they did not, technically speaking, dissent from the formularies, teaching and discipline of the Church of England. In this essay, Dissenters include Congregationalists (as the old Independents came to be known), Baptists, Presbyterians and Unitarians. It is with these churches that we shall be concerned. Now we define them more closely and put them in their historical setting.

Congregationalists were distinguished by two fundamental beliefs. In the first place, as the name implies, they believed that final authority rested in the whole Church or congregation, and not in the Minister or Bishop. This necessarily implied that the Minister was subservient to the whole Church, in a way that was quite alien to Presbyterianism and the Church of England. Secondly, mid-eighteenth century Congregationalists adhered to a strict Calvinism, and more especially to a high doctrine of election and predestination. This implied a belief in God's initiative in salvation, and therefore discouraged missionary and proselytizing activity. On Christological questions—i.e. on questions about the nature of the Person of Christ—the bulk of Congregationalists were orthodox, that is they followed the doctrine of the Established Church. But a significant minority, among them the famous Belsham, espoused heterodox views and became Arians or Unitarians, teaching that Christ was an exemplar but not divine. The Christological disputes of the mid-eighteenth century went far towards sapping the energies and intellect of the Church and did nothing to bring it into immediate contact with the political and social questions that exercised Wesley, and, to a lesser extent, Whitefield.

The perils of Socianism had weakened orthodox Dissent by the middle of the eighteenth century. Still subject to the penalties imposed at the Restoration, orthodox Dissenters were distinguished for neither their numbers nor their energy. Watts and Doddridge were more concerned with keeping their congregations in being than with extending their sphere of influence.[1] But the Evangelical Revival brought a new sense of urgency, and with it a new dynamism. Men like John Edwards at Leeds and Jonathan Scott at Lancaster had absorbed the theology and zeal of the Evangelicals from the Methodists or the Established Church, and brought it to the flagging Independents. This cross-fertilization was important because it brought to the Independent theology a dilution of the Calvinism that had been its distinguishing feature throughout the century. By showing that a doctrine of election was compatible with a general invitation to believe and be saved, the moderate Calvinists, like both Jonathan and James Scott in the eighteenth century and Thomas Scales early in the nineteenth, impressed upon the denomination its duty to present the Gospel to the world.

This could only be achieved with some moderation of the independency of individual churches. Although there had traditionally been an element of interdependency in the denomination's scheme of government, this had become very weak in the eighteenth century and was confined to occasional meetings for prayer and debate. By the end of the eighteenth century the principle of association on a more permanent basis was widely conceded. Indicative of this was the meeting held at Tintwistle in Cheshire in 1798 'for the purpose of promoting a more friendly intercourse among ministers and Christian brethren and of consulting together for the wider extension of the gospel'.[2] Three years later an Itinerant Society was founded to evangelize the North of England.

The development of a less rigorous form of Calvinism and the

---

[1] *Evangelical Magazine* (1836), p. 182.
[2] Quoted in W. Gordon Robinson, *A History of the Lancashire Congregational Union, 1806–1956* (Manchester, 1955), p. 25.

parallel establishment of a more articulated organization produced significant changes in the whole outlook and nature of the Church. It is easy to exaggerate the extent of these developments by 1830, but certainly the ethos of the Congregationalism of the 1830s and '40s was very far removed from that of mid-eighteenth century Independency. The latter was defensive, other worldly, bourgeois and dull: the former missionizing, socially involved, ready to flirt with radicalism and exciting. With greater co-operation among individual Churches and a readiness to indulge in the hurly-burly of aggressive proselytizing in urban and rural slums, there came a new vision of the Church's relationship with the rest of the world.

The Congregationalists, then, had become intensely aware of the existential implications of their faith by the 1840s. They had left behind them the debilitating theological logic-chopping that had characterized so much of their writing, thinking and preach-ing in the mid-eighteenth century, and if the full yield from the new theology and the new social catholicity was not to be drawn until later, there were already pressures acting on the Church from both within and without, making it take a greater cognisance of the social order and a more serious view of its own responsibilities vis-à-vis that order.

The same is broadly true of the Baptists. The Baptist Church was even more fissiparous than the Independent, but each splinter group remained faithful to the theological *raison d'être* of the parent body, an unyielding insistence on believers' (as opposed to infant) baptism, and the emphasis, implied to a large extent by a high Calvinism, on a fully conscious decision and committal by the baptised. The two main bodies of Baptist teaching were the General Baptists and the Particular Baptists.

Both had been weakened by the problems of Christology posed by Arianism, and the former gradually merged into Unitarianism. Although sharing his connexional form of organization and his Arminianism, the General Baptists were not attracted to Wesley because of his failure to recognise the futility of infant Sprinkling. But Methodist influence on the Baptists was not for that reason vitiated. The tradition of the General Baptists was only saved by the New Connection of the General Baptists which was almost wholly Methodist in its inspiration. Although the New Connec-tion maintained some of the archaisms of the old Assembly, it was more aware of the problems created by urbanization and became relatively strong in the Midlands, Lancashire and Yorkshire.

The Particular Baptists were led by their hyper-Calvinism to a position which could be easily represented as Antinomian, and although there were no Antinomians in the Ministry, some congregations were affected by this heresy.[1] As high Calvinists and even Supralapsarians (teaching that evil existed before the Fall), the Particular Baptists had little in common with Wesley's Arminianism. A further factor insulating the Calvinists from Wesley was their strong emphasis on independency and the autonomy of the congregation. The initial impulse came to the Particular Baptists, therefore, not from Wesley but from Whitefield who was himself a Calvinist. Although some, like William Gadsby, adhered to their hyper-Calvinism (and became the Strict and Particular Baptists), under the influence of Fuller and Robert Hall, senior, the Particular Baptists moderated their Calvinism. The two classics of moderation, Hall's *Help to Zion's Travellers* (1781) and Fuller's *The Gospel Worthy of All Acceptation* (1785) both showed that the doctrine of election was not inconsistent with missionary activity.

In the organization of the Church this had a profound effect. It led not only to the organization of the Baptist Missionary Society and Carey's visit to Serampore, but also, partly as a result of the foreign missions, a greater awareness of the need for and value of home missions. But this could only be effected by a far greater degree of inter-church co-operation. The Particular Baptists were, therefore, induced to relax their insistence on complete congregational autonomy and experiment with forms of association. It was no coincidence that the meeting out of which the General Union of Baptist Churches arose in 1812 was originally organized to raise money for the Missionary Society. Towards the end of the period, then, the Baptists like the Independents were developing new denominational organs, which, while safeguarding the autonomy of the congregations in local affairs, provided for a greater degree of mutual support at home and overseas.

A number of reasons militated against the Baptists becoming quite as socially articulate as the Congregationalists. First, their Ministers were less well educated. Second, their ecclesiastical

---

[1] Antinomianism is the belief that grace so abounds that moral law is irrelevant.

system, with its formal and formidable token of membership, made membership of the Church so central in the reference of an individual as to rob his social, political or economic circumstances of much of their reality. Third, their Calvinistic doctrine of Providence survived the dilution of their doctrine of election. 'How must the good man rejoice when amidst all the changes of the world and the disasters of time, and the vicissitudes of his own life or feelings, he remembers that the Lord omnipotent reigneth!'[1] That this was not merely another Scriptural reinforcement of the *status quo*, but rather a deeply held theological position, is suggested by William Pendred's admonition to Baptists to accept their political disabilities in the same spirit. 'Let patience and industry, then, unite to sustain whatever burdens the legislature may impose, and whatever public grievances divine providence may inflict.'[2] Fourth, this naïve doctrine led Baptists to an equally naïve view of the source of misery and poverty in the world.[3] 'God and angels are holy and happy; and happy because they are holy, Devils and wicked men are miserable: and they are wicked because unholy. Good men are holy and therefore happy.'[4] This analysis necessarily led to a 'spiritualizing' of the real problems of society—a process that bedevilled much social thinking and action throughout the nineteenth century. Fifth, there was a deeply entrenched prejudice against ministerial preoccupation with political and social problems. 'To read critiques, of . . . works on science and political economy written by ministers and unconnected with any moral or religious purpose is truly lamentable and can leave but one conviction in the minds of those who piously reflect on the state and character of their authors. Happily . . . such instances are rare, if they exist at all.'[5]

Although these factors explain why the Baptists were less to the forefront in the socio-economic debates of the period, they should not be taken to imply that all social concern was stifled in the Baptist Church. The home missions revealed much to

[1] *Baptist Magazine* (1827), p. 162.
[2] W. Pendred, *The Duty of Christians to Seek the Peace and Welfare of the Community* (Halifax, 1797), p. 18.
[3] This was by no means, of course, a uniquely Baptist view.
[4] T. H. Hudson, *Christian Socialism explained and enforced* . . . (1839), p. 194. The title of this work is misleading. It is in reality a prolonged and rather silly attack on Owen, supported by a mass of scriptural quotation. 'Socialism', in any normal sense, is not mentioned.
[5] *Baptist Magazine* (1823), pp. 282–3.

polite Baptist society about the condition of the lower orders. As we shall see below, like the Unitarians, some Baptists reacted violently against the traditional Whig liberalism of the denomination when they were thus brought face to face with the basic human needs in the urban areas of the thirties and forties.

The history of the Presbyterian and Unitarian Churches can be noticed more briefly. We shall only be interested in Presbyterianism to the extent to which it contributed to Unitarianism. From Presbyterianism English Unitarianism inherited three features. The first was a belief, somewhat modified by Priestley and his followers, that the minister, as presbyter, was the source of authority in the Church. The second was a greater intellectual awareness than any other denomination could boast; the third was the loyalty of a disproportionate number of the upper classes —some landed gentry, but more usually wealthy merchants and bankers. Thus of the Presbyterian-Unitarians of Nottingham at the time of the secession of the Unitarians, their historian says: 'The members . . . were generally of a description superior to what most provincial towns are capable of affording: men of cultivated understandings and of great moral worth.'[1]

These special features, as well as a very considerable proportion of their members and property, the Unitarian Church took from the Presbyterians. Arianism, the belief that Jesus was not a divine saviour but only an exemplar, had an ancient history, but only established itself as a regular Church in England in the later years of the eighteenth century. Hitherto, the English Arians had been distinguished not only by their leisured scepticism, but also by their 'slowness, . . . stiffness, . . . ease and . . . shuffling'.[2] But the fusion of Presbyterian organization and academic ability, Unitarian theology, heterodox Anglican influence, and heterodox Independent energy brought a new dynamism and coherence to the English Unitarian Church. By the end of the century, thanks largely to Priestley, Unitarianism was provided with a debased congregationalism, a clear-cut, dogmatic theology and a political radicalism and utilitarianism. Between them these not only bonded together the diverse elements of which the Church was composed, but also gave it an influence and leadership that were quite disproportionate to its numerical strength.

[1] B. Carpenter, *Some Account of the Original Introduction of Presbyterianism into Nottingham with a brief history . . . of High Pavement* (Nottingham, 1862(?)), p. 167.
[2] A. H. Drysdale, *A History of English Presbyterianism* (London, 1889), p. 537.

However, despite the excitement caused by the Unitarians' support of the French Revolutionaries, by the end of the Napoleonic Wars the denomination was characterized chiefly by a spiritual dullness. The Romantic wing of Unitarianism, which had continued its championship of the Revolution after the first blush of idealism, had caught the full force of the backwash of anti-Jacobinism. In the period of repression after 1815 the theological dogmatism of Priestley and Belsham combined with their utilitarianism to drain the church of vigour. The legal difficulties of open trusts that culminated in the Wolverhampton and Lady Hewley Cases added to the burden. The accession of the General Baptists brought numerical improvement but some sociological conflict rendered worse by the congregational government that Priestley had propagated.

It was against the spiritual deadness which these factors produced that the Transcendentalists reacted. 'They burst into a forgotten chamber of the soul', said Martineau of the sermons of Channing,[1] who, with Emerson, provided the English Transcendentalists with so much of their inspiration.[2] But it was an emotional inspiration that took until the 1850s to crystallize into a consistent corpus of doctrine. Although by no means all the Unitarian churches espoused this new mode of religious expression, it gradually became both more influential and more widespread, especially after 1845, for it was more faithful to the original ethos of Presbyterian Arianism than the Priestleyan dogmatism which had shackled the denomination for half a century.

III

In each of the chief denominations of Dissent, then, there were inherent sociological conflicts as a result of the new theology and missionary initiatives. In orthodox Dissent, home and foreign missions were undertaken as fast as the disjointed organizations of the Churches would allow. By the 1830s these were bearing fruit throughout orthodox Dissent, with the result that the social pattern of Dissent was altered radically, especially in the urban areas. For the home missions, though not outstandingly successful

[1] Quoted in H. Gow, *The Unitarians* (London, 1928), p. 112.
[2] R. Wellek, 'Emerson and German Philosophy', *New England Quarterly* (1943).

in themselves, brought working class members to the Churches and, perhaps more important, wider perspectives to the traditional membership. This process of widening the social appeal of the orthodox Dissent can be traced from a number of pieces of indirect evidence.

The topography of chapel buildings in many of the growing towns is often instructive. The Dissenting chapels of the seventeenth century were frequently built on the periphery of the towns to avoid the attention of the mob. Later the pompous chapels of the city centres were built in the earlier decades of the nineteenth. By the middle of the century, the rash of small daughter or mission chapels was being built in the slums.

The rationale of this pattern of chapel building, the widened social appeal of the Calvinist churches, led to the adoption of new policies in the economic organization of the churches, which is itself further evidence of the attempt of Dissent to extend the social basis of its membership. Not only was the number of free seats greatly increased; but, perhaps more important, more seats at rentals designed to be within the reach of all but the lowest paid workers were provided.

Thus the economy of the individual chapel as well as of the Church at large came to rest upon *both* the old, monied, mercantile families *and* the new aristocracy of labour.

The attempts made by the Baptists and Independents to tap the resources of the poorer members of the congregation is symptomatic of the reorientation in their theology towards the unchurched masses. The Penny-a-Week Societies and Home Mission Societies that sprang into life in the 1830s and '40s, admittedly owing much to the Wesleyan Methodist example, illustrate the new approach of the Calvinists to their poor—'We are perhaps too apt to be looking . . . to the rich, as if they were to do all. No doubt they are bound to set an example and to contribute largely and liberally: but let us not despise the poor and their offerings'.[1] While it would be unhistorical to imply any kind of economic determinism, it remains true that the broadening financial support of Calvinism necessarily brought with it a demand that the traditional payers of the piper should no longer exclusively call the tune.

As Drysdale remarks: 'Independent Churches could and did

[1] *Baptist Magazine* (1841), p. 659; *Evangelical Magazine* (1840), p. 33.

operate directly and decidedly on their ministers from within: purely and fully-equipped Presbyterian Churches can do so yet more effectively by the control of Church courts from without . . . In the Presbyterian Churches there had crept in the evils of both *family patronage* and of *trusteeism* . . . These evil symptoms were not confined to the Presbyterians. They affected all denominations . . .'[1]

It was not, however, merely that Orthodox Dissent came to depend financially on the skilled and semi-skilled industrial workers. Consciously borrowing from Wesleyan Methodism, the Calvinists established a power-structure which gave increasing influence within the Church to this new social group. But, like the Methodists, the Calvinists found that, having used organizational involvement as an adhesive bait for lower class members and having thus admitted them to positions of power within the organization, it was impossible to muzzle their insistence that some traditional attitudes be drastically modified.

In the Unitarian Church, these sociological divisions are more difficult to identify and substantiate until the Transcendentalists heightened the inherent conflicts already within the Church. Unlike the Calvinists, the Unitarians were never much concerned with missionary activity, and therefore its feed-back effect which was so formative in the Calvinist Churches was minimal. Nonetheless, the aristocratic and patrician exclusiveness of the Unitarians was moderated by the influx of the General Baptists after 1815, although it is easy to exaggerate the extent to which the two bodies effectively fused. It was only when the Transcendentalists brought to the mainstream of Unitarianism a new radicalism of thought and action that conflict was inevitable with the entrenched patrician interest in the Church. Such dissidence within the Church as is apparent before 1840 is the result as much of the emphasis in the Church on the rational analysis of problems as of any obvious class conflict.

IV

In each Church, then, we can detect social divisions creating inhibiting tensions within the denomination. We describe now

[1] Drysdale, op. cit., pp. 509, 511, 527.

some of the issues which revealed most clearly the effects of these divisions on social ethics and dogmatics.

The first example is the attitude of the Independents to the Ten Hour Movement. To propitiate the manufacturer element in the Church, many ministers condemned the Factory Acts. In Leeds, Hamilton spoke in public against them,[1] and in the *Leeds Mercury*, Baines represented a strong Liberal-Radical resistance to state interference of any kind,[2] so much so that as Michael Sadler wrote to the Duke of Newcastle in 1832 with ill-concealed glee: '. . . the Mercury Newspaper was burnt in the open street . . . and the same night the effigy of the editor (Mr Baines) was carried in procession through the principal streets . . . proceeding to Mr Baines before whose door it was burnt amidst the execrations of about 10,000 persons'.[3] That this was typical of the majority of the Independent Church in the North is suggested by the lack of response to a letter in the *Evangelical Magazine* in 1833 demanding to know 'what the Ministers and leading persons, both among Churchmen and Dissenters, in the great towns of Yorkshire and Lancashire have been doing, that we have been kept in ignorance of this iniquitous treatment of the children of the humbler classes.'[4] Hamilton and both the elder and younger Baines denied categorically much of the evidence taken by the Sadler Committee, and regarded conditions in the towns as no worse and in most instances much better, than in the country.[5] But Hamilton did not deny the existence of child labour. He thought it justifiable. 'Their probable sphere of life is that of industry and to industry they should be trained. Their education, however scanty, depends upon the price of their industry. It may be stern necessity . . . The fabric must be produced.'[6]

But alongside this seeming denial of the whole spirit of protest against urban and factory conditions which the movement embodied lies a series of concessions that seem to justify just such a protest. Hamilton, for instance, pressed for better conditions

---

[1] *Leeds Mercury*, February 4th, 1832.

[2] See D. Read, *Press and People, 1790–1850* (London, 1961), pp. 116–36.

[3] MS letter, Leeds, 4th May, 1832, in Newcastle Collection, University Library, Nottingham.

[4] *Evangelical Magazine* (1833), p. 65.

[5] Hamilton, *The Institutions of Popular Education* (London, 1845), pp. 41–3. This major contribution to Congregationalists' social thinking may be regarded as typical of the more progressive elements in the denomination, for it was awarded the Manchester Prize in 1844.

[6] Hamilton, *Institutions*, sup. cit., p. 56.

and hours of work for labourers; relief of the boredom and drudgery of much of the labour; and for a more sympathetic and sensitive approach to the problems of labour by employers.[1] Bull claimed that he, Hamilton, was in favour of the movement.[2] There is no evidence of public support of the movement by Hamilton and the clandestine nature of his support, if it existed at all, is indicative of the embarrassment of Hamilton's position. Ely, another Independent minister, joined him in condemning, or at least questioning, the system of distribution which produced such startling inequalities of conditions.[3] The 'necessary diversity in social condition was aggravated by the greed of the employers as a class'.[4] But to put a statutory limit on the working hours of the artisan was, therefore, to deny him the right to diminish this diversity. In Hamilton's view, 'to restrict his hours of labour by any legislative enactment is to oppress him. It is to sell away his birthright, his capital, his all'.[5] Such a distorted paradox is evidence enough of the contrary pressure at work on the Independents.

The attitude to combinations reveals the same duality. Parliamentary candidates soliciting the votes of Independents were to commit themselves to 'preventing . . . all injurious and selfish combinations on the part either of the employed or employers'.[6] Where combinations of employers already exerted pressure on the livelihood of employees, there Hamilton at least regarded combinations of artisans justifiable. For 'the freedom of labour and the freedom of combination are not more than sufficient equipoise to the weight of counter influences.'[7] Yet Hamilton condemned strikes, without the threat of which as an ultimate sanction combinations of artisans must be nearly powerless. 'If the workman asks for what is incompatible with the progress of mechanical improvement and mercantile liberty, he asks . . . for the destruction of his class.'[8] Hamilton further represented strikes, not as morally wrong, but as ill advised on the ground that they tended to reduce wages.[9]

---

[1] Hamilton, *Institutions*, sup. cit., pp. 7, 20, 29.
[2] G. S. Bull, *The Duty of the Ministers of the Gospel to plead the Cause of the Industrious and Indigenous Labourers of the Country*, n.p. 1833, p.2.
[3] *Leeds Mercury*, 14th Dec., 1839.
[4] *Evangelical Magazine* (1842), p. 28.
[5] Hamilton', *Institutions*, sup. cit., p. 108.
[6] *Congregational Magazine* (1832), p. 580.
[7] Hamilton', *Institutions*, sup. cit., p. 27.
[8] Ibid., p. 17.
[9] Ibid., p. 20.

In the Baptist Church, the Ten Hour Movement received more articulate support. The *Baptist Magazine* at least supported the aspirations of the working classes. 'We earnestly hope that all our congregations will immediately adopt petitions to the Legislature, praying that the Bill, to be brought in by Lord Ashley, may be adopted to confine the hours of labour to ten hours per day . . . and that no children under nine years shall in future be employed.'[1]

But the significant fact is that to the leaders of the movement, this articulate support seemed no more than lip-service. Oastler declared that 'the poor "dependent" parson dared not even say that his soul was his own; he dared not to denounce the curse of God against them (millowners who exploited child-labour), but was forced to daub these impious wretches with untempered mortar!'[2] That the wealthy Baptists evaded and opposed the Factory Acts was obvious. '. . . These Liberal Dissenting deaconized blood-hounds used before they put the breaking-bits on, to work the poor infant slaves till within twenty minutes of the Sabbath morn—and as soon as the clock struck twelve on Sunday night the slaves were at their mills again! But Sunday was a holy day! Oh! How they prayed and wept and canted! Six days they lied, and cheated and murdered, but the seventh they did keep holy—excepting that the mechanics and joiners and chimney-sweeps were all Sabbath day long as busy as bees, mending, repairing and sweeping in their mills!'[3] Even the *Baptist Magazine* was forced to admit that there were occasions when the Minister was powerless to correct the wealthy in his congregation.[4] To do so would be to court financial disaster.

The historian of the Unitarian contribution to social progress, R. V. Holt, has amply demonstrated that the Unitarian church was also split by the Factory Movement. It was a three-way division. On the one hand, there was the distinction between the manufacturing and non-manufacturing interest. In each group

[1] *Baptist Magazine* (1833), p. 131.
[2] R. Oastler, *The Unjust Judge or the Sign of the Judge's Skin. A Letter to George Goodman, Esq., Mayor of Leeds* (Leeds, 1836), p. 9. The use of the term 'parson' is misleading. Oastler was writing of the Baptist ministers.
[3] Ibid. Oastler made the same kind of attack on the lace-manufacturers of Nottingham in 1839, for which he was firmly rebuked by the Whig-Dissent controlled *Nottingham Review*. See J. C. Weller, *The Revival of Religion in Nottingham 1780–1850*. University of Nottingham B.D. Thesis 1957, pp. 243–5.
[4] *Baptist Magazine* (1842), p. 237.

there was a strong minority siding with the opposition. Against such manufacturers as Mark Philips, Edward Stutt, John Bowring and R. H. Greg, warmly against the Movement in general and Ashley's Bill of 1833 in particular, there were such atypical figures as John Fielden, whose work for the Movement has probably been underestimated. A more passive element sided in general with Fielden, although it refused to become as involved as he. Thus the Nottingham Unitarian Morley thought 'the beauty of the stocking trade . . . is its domestic character', and with many other Dissenting merchants regretted the coming of the factories.[1] On the other hand, many of the non-manufacturers, ministers, scholars and gentlemen of leisure, were equally opposed to the Factory Acts, although in general this socio-economic group favoured some supervision of child labour. Holt points out that there are some shreds of evidence that the small artisan element in the Unitarian Church was firmly in support of the Movement, and thus in direct conflict with a large, perhaps preponderant, group of the wealthy members of the Church.[2] Reflecting thus uncertainty and conflict of pressures, *The Inquirer* gave denominational opinion no clear lead, but represented both points of view throughout the 1830s.

The degree of disunity and ambivalence thus shown by the three leading Dissenting bodies is the more surprising in light of the fact that the Factory Acts came so near the interests of those very classes with whom Dissent is usually glibly identified. That such dualism existed is evidence of the influence exerted by the new theology and its elaboration in the missionary situation. A slightly different but equally striking example of the way in which the theological reawakening of Dissent produced within its ranks conflicting forces is the attitude to the New Poor Law of 1834. Bull met opposition from Independent ministers.[3] John Hanson, Independent Minister of Loxley, near Sheffield, was 'deprived of a great part of his accustomed scanty stipend, for having opposed the New Poor Law',[4] by Dr Pye Smith, who was connected with the Baines family by marriage, and who was one of the administrators of the Regium Donum. Hamilton declared

---

[1] *Report of the Select Committee on the Stoppage of Wages* (1856), p. 386.
[2] R. V. Holt, *The Unitarian Contribution to Social Progress in England*, 2nd revised edition (London, 1952), p. 190.
[3] Bull, op. cit., p. 2.
[4] Roberts, op. cit., p. 30.

the usual political-economist's maxim that 'he who will not work ought not to eat',[1] and thus upheld the cessation of the Speenhamland system and the introduction of the principle of less eligibility. 'It is not contended that the able bodied are, by any just construction of the law, entitled to a fare of comfort and abundance . . . which the self supporting cottager does not know.'[2] Large scale out-door relief was condemned as conducive to 'the pauper spirit, that with abject meanness cares not whose bread it eats, so only it may be had'.[3]

Yet at the same time Hamilton demanded the right of a subsistence for all. 'The luxurious diet is not the due of any: decent subsistence is the claim of all. . . . There is no power to relegate the meanest outcast from this national provision.'[4] In phraseology strikingly like that of Bull, he claimed that 'the whole population of this country is this country's trust. No man has home, above the meanest hut, but that home is mortgaged for the support of his poorer compatriots.'[5] He laid claim to relief as of right. 'No man can be an intruder in the world. . . . His birth gives right of place and provision in it.'[6] He and Ely were emphatic in their rejection of the Malthusian hypothesis, and although their grounds of refutation were unsophisticated, they refused to regard 'the labouring poor' as 'an excrescence or a surplus or an evil'.[7] But although there is a right of provision and although all classes have a claim to a share of the national product, 'labour, like every trading interest, is best promoted when it is least indulged. It must hold and abide its market. The swaddling bands of a mistaken kindness and custody only cramp its energies and frustrate its rewards.'[8] In this teaching either social group would find something palatable.

To a lesser degree, perhaps, the same ambivalence can be found in Baptist teaching. Even in the correspondence of the *Baptist Magazine*, the mainstay of Baptist orthodoxy, there are some traces of bitterness against the New Poor Law. A correspondent

---

[1] Hamilton, *Institutions*, sup. cit., p. 7.
[2] Hamilton, *Institutions*, sup. cit., p. 14.
[3] *Congregational Magazine* (1835), p. 539.
[4] Hamilton, *Institutions*, sup. cit., p. 14.
[5] Ibid., p. 13, cf. J. C. Gill, *Ten Hours Parson* (London, 1959), p. 156.
[6] Ibid., p. 4.
[7] Ibid., p. 25, cf. Hamilton (ed.), *Posthumous Works of Revd. John Ely*, pp. 383–426, esp. 413, 415.
[8] Ibid., p. 14.

in 1836 declared that the law was 'framed in an unmerciful spirit',[1] and an editorial comments on the widespread anxiety in Baptist churches over the Law.[2] Even its apologists were forced to admit that in some respects, especially in its separation of man from wife, the law was harsh.[3] In the industrial North and perhaps too, in the rural areas where the Baptist churches were often numerous, it is highly probable that the lower class Baptists were opposed to the Law. Yet the preponderant weight of Baptist teaching was warmly in favour of it. 'It is working great and obvious benefits to the community and will especially conduce to elevate the moral and social condition of the labouring classes.'[4] In the North, Bull, Oastler and Roberts were dismayed to find little support and sometimes open hostility from Baptist ministers in their opposition to the enforcement of the law in the North. 'Oh ye . . . innumerable Dissenting ministers of every denomination throughout the Kingdom, why are ye, with some half-dozen exceptions, silent all? . . .'[5]

In the case of the Unitarians, the situation is more complex, though the divisive effect of the exploration of new theological frontiers is more obvious. From Priestley's teaching, the denomination inherited first the assumption of the necessary harmony of class interest and second the ideal of assisted self-help. How far Unitarianism can be identified with Utilitarianism is difficult to determine, but certainly after 1818 the *Monthly Repository* was closely in line with the leading Utilitarians of the day. It was no accident that Manchester was the spiritual home of both. Even the *Christian Reformer*, hitherto a wayward Unitarian journal, ceased to criticize the Political Economists and in 1833 was still convinced of the harmony of classes. The *Inquirer* was closely aligned with the Manchester School, and accordingly gave its support to the New Poor Law. To the more extreme exponents of this view, it was clear that the laws of political economy as much as the laws of science were the laws of God. To them the incompatibility of social reconciliation and the laws of political economy was apparent not real. If the laws of political economy

---

[1] *Baptist Magazine* (1836), p. 225.
[2] Ibid., p. 236.
[3] Ibid., pp. 341–2.
[4] Ibid., p. 341.
[5] Samuel Roberts, *A Solemn Appeal to the Ministers of the Gospel of Every Denomination on the Subject of the Poor Laws* (Sheffield, 1837), p. 11, cf. Bull, op. cit., p. 2.

were faithfully followed, the ends foreshadowed in the Gospels would be realised. Thus Thom tried to prove that the laws of the Gospels *were* the laws of political economy.

Contrasting with those Unitarians who, even after the disenchantment caused by the publication of Bentham's *Deontology* in 1834, followed the Utilitarians on most of the social issues of the day, were, not only the more radical wing of the 'orthodox' Unitarians which found expression in the *Christian Teacher*, but, much more, the Transcendentalists. Compare the usual Utilitarian defence of the New Poor Law with the emotional outbursts of some of the leading Transcendentalists. Thus, Wicksteed said he was 'firmly convinced . . . that a more equitable arrangement of the commercial intercourse and laws of this country is absolutely necessary to its continued, or rather to its restored well-being . . . the poor are starving for lack of bread'.[1] Martineau and Tayler were content to deny the complete freedom of the individual in the name of 'the rights of labour, the rights of the poor, the right of the industrious to be fed and clothed out of the fruits of his industry'.[2] That this amounted to a denial of the omnipotence of the laws of political economy does not appear to have embarrassed them. Social reconciliation was the great aim of their teaching, just as it was, so they pointed out, the great aim of the Gospels.[3] Only when political and social institutions 'become Christian in deed and truth'[4] can this aim be achieved. 'I regard it', wrote Beard, the most telling of the prophets of the radical wing, 'as a divine interference in order to assert the rightful claims of the poor and adjust the inequalities created by partial and exclusive legislation.'[5] But interference would not always be necessary. 'The Gospel will eventually supersede all law, by making each man a law to himself.'[6] Morality and benevolence will establish a freedom as yet undreamed of. 'The great aim of the religion of Jesus (is to) substitute moral and spiritual power for the lower, not to say depraving, appliances of force and restraint.'[7] Beard shared with Priestley the conviction that society was moving towards the

[1] Quoted in A. Brockett, *Nonconformity in Exeter, 1650–1875* (Manchester, 1962), p. 144.
[2] Tayler, Thom, Wicksteed and J. Martineau edited the *Prospective Review* from 1845. This then became the medium of this wing of Unitarian opinion.
[3] Ibid., p. 762, cf. pp. 835–6.
[4] Ibid., p. 762.
[5] Ibid.
[6] Ibid., p. 833.
[7] Ibid., p. 836.

ideal.[1] 'The minister of Jesus supersedes the executioner. The process . . . has hitherto been but slow, and it is not easy to find marked instances of the change: but the attentive observer of the state of society in this country will not have failed to have noticed that no small portion of modern . . . legislation has consisted in enduring the bands which past ages have fabricated. Every year this work of emancipation is being done . . .'[2]

Two further examples of this conflict within Dissent may be taken from individual denominations. Perhaps the clearest illustration of the internal tensions of the Baptist churches as reflected in their social teaching lies in the discussion of wealth and poverty. We have already seen that the Baptists had a strong sense of Providence. To the problem of individual poverty the answer was the same as the Wesleyans'—that in His wisdom, God has assigned this lot to that individual. But to the moral question of the existence of class structure the Baptist ministry gave two contradictory replies. Hudson, the author of *Christian Socialism*—a work whose content belies its title—denied that Christianity destroyed 'natural and unavoidable diversities in a social community'. Rather it sanctified them.[3] Diametrically opposed was the radical view, best expressed by the Leeds Baptist Minister, John Giles. In a fiery speech to a meeting composed largely of Chartists, he denied the existence and ethical defensibility of the class structure. 'Something had been said that day about different classes of the people. He, for one, repudiated the idea of different classes in British society (loud applause). Were they not all brothers? (Applause) Were they not all Englishmen? (Applause) Were they not all, professedly at least, freemen? Nay, he would ask were they not all men? (Loud applause) Then away with the absurd idea of upper and middle and lower classes! (Tremendous cheers) . . .'[4] In the denomination there thus coexisted an extreme radicalism that would appeal to the lower classes and an old Whiggism leavened with liberalism that would be palatable to the wealthy merchants.

In the Unitarian Church, the French Revolution itself was the subject of heated debate. In Exeter, the Minister, himself as much

[1] Ibid., p. 831.
[2] Ibid. (1844), p. 836.
[3] T. H. Hudson: *Christian Socialism explained and enforced and compared with infidel fellowship, especially as propounded by Robert Owen* (London, 1839), p. 156.
[4] *Leeds Mercury*, 20th May, 1843.

in favour of the Revolution in 1793 as in 1759, wrote: 'Most of the Dissenters in this part of the Country have joined with the members of the Establishment in making professions of attachment to the Constitution, and of their abhorrence of all attempts to overturn it by seditious writings. In the list of subscribers I have often been mortified to see names which I little expected to behold there . . .'[1] The struggles that followed in Exeter were paralleled in Leeds, Manchester and even in Birmingham.[2]

On more specifically social issues, we have already seen that the main body of Unitarians was committed to an uncritical utilitarianism. Early in the century child labour was condoned,[3] inequality was upheld,[4] the necessary connection between poverty and misery was denied[5] and sceptism of the education of the lower classes was encouraged.[6] Contentment was urged with a thoroughness that the best of Wesleyans could admire,[7] and the activities of the merchant warmly praised.[8] 'How, in serving himself, does the merchant greatly serve society! How wonderful is the scheme of things produced by the desire for gain—the same motive which stimulates the industry and talents of every class.'[9]

But this was only the predominant tone. Especially after the accession to the Unitarian body of the General Baptists there appeared a section of opinion opposed to the doctrines of the wealthy commercial cliques. To these, the adherence of numbers of poorer members from the General Baptists might have been an embarrassment, for the latter were unlikely to have much sympathy with the predominant social conservatism. Under Aspland the *Monthly Repository* assumed a piecemeal social radicalism. Wider education with more liberal curricula was canvassed. Penal reform was a common theme and the abolition of slavery

---

[1] Quoted in Brockett, op. cit., p. 144.

[2] See Brockett, op. cit. passim, for a full account of the position in Exeter.

[3] W. Wood, *A Sermon Preached at Birmingham, on 9th June, 1805 . . . in aid of a Collection for the Protestant Dissenters' Charity School* (Leeds, 1805), p. 24, cf. p. 26.

[4] Ibid., pp. 6–7, 12, cf. Thomas Johnstone, *A Sermon Recommending Benevolence and Charity* (Sheffield, 1793), p. 6.

[5] Ibid., p. 7.

[6] Thomas Jervis, *The Enquiry of Talents, and the Reward of Active Virtue and Benevolence* (London, 1813), pp. 16–17.

[7] See J. Bowden, *Sermons* (Leeds, 1804). The titles of some of these Sermons are 'The Unreasonableness of Discontent', 'An Unprofitableness of Discontent', and 'The Vision of Godliness with Contentment'.

[8] *Inquirer* (1846) 224, p. 647. Quoted in Sellers: *Political and Social Attitudes of Representative English Unitarians* (B.Litt. Thesis, Oxford, 1956), p. 114.

[9] *Christian Teacher* (1839), pp. 280–89, cf. 1844, p. 280, and *Christian Reformer* 1844, p. 1044.

was accorded generous space. With this the commercial oligarchy could have little disagreement. But the Malthusian hypothesis was attacked and rejected,[1] and capitalism was assailed.[2] Co-operation,[3] Owenite socialism[4] and a more even distribution of property were endorsed.[5]

These examples of conflict, disunity and ambivalence in the social dogmatics of both individual denominations and Dissent as a whole must not be allowed to create a false impression. There were issues on which almost universal agreement was evident. The Independents united with all Dissenters[6] to attack the Corn Laws. 'Competition, whatever may be its inconveniences, is an unmixed good in comparison with any stagnation in human fortunes.'[7] Repeal was urged in every denominational medium. 'It may be said that the over-trading of past years has occasioned the present reaction upon our manufacturing population: or that the state of the foreign markets has lessened the demand for many of our articles of commerce: but will it be denied that the existing pressure falls with disproportionate severity upon the manufacturing interests of the community? Or can it be affirmed with truth that the landed interests are suffering anything like the same amount of distress and embarrassment as now prevails in the spinning mills and warehouses of Manchester, Glasgow, Paisley and other places?'[8] 'Benefiting no class but the aristocracy of the soil', the Corn Laws were to be repealed in order to prevent the continued counteraction of 'the merciful designs of that Providence which proportions the supplies to the necessities of the human race, considered as one great family, whose interests in the eye of heaven, are essentially one'.[9] The juxtaposition of the two principal deleterious effects of the Corn Laws is significant. They 'limit commerce (and) increase to a ruinous extent the price of provisions'.[10]

Their repeal features in most non-ecclesiastical writings of Independent ministers, and sermons contain many explicit or

---

[1] *Monthly Repository* (1817), XII, pp. 471–4.
[2] *Monthly Repository* (1821), XVI, pp. 88–101.
[3] *Monthly Repository* (1817), XII, p. 510.
[4] *Monthly Repository* (1823), XVII, pp. 450–7.
[5] Ibid.
[6] But, interestingly, hardly any Wesleyan Methodists.
[7] R. W. Hamilton, *Institutions*, sup cit., p. 19.
[8] *Evangelical Magazine* (1842), p. 28.
[9] Ibid.
[10] Ibid.

implicit references to their vexatious effects.[1] Like the quotations given above, nearly every mention of the subject emphasizes the extent to which repeal was a cause to which all classes, at least in manufacturing areas, could assent.[2] The great Manchester meeting of clergy in support of the Anti-Corn Law League in 1844 was symptomatic of the universality of this line of thought. The Transcendentalists naturally emphasized the effect repeal would have on the standard of living of the poor, and considered the lower incomes which this would entail for land-owners a feeble counter-argument. Thus Wicksteed said 'he was sick of hearing of the burdens of the rich—the burdens of the land—in face of starvation and want for the poor. This land was indeed becoming a burden, and was beginning to be like a mill-stone about their necks. The very land which nature intended for this support was, by an artifice in legislation, by a vile and wicked sophism, becoming a limiter of their supplies and an instrument of their starvation'.[3]

Similarly, the need for improved educational facilities was admitted by each denomination. Sabbatarianism, tee-totalism, penal reform, saving clubs, cottage gardens and all the stock-in-trade of early Victorian social improvers found greater or less support in each denomination. Even the strife-torn, undogmatic Unitarians could find some areas of agreement, chief among them the need for a drastic overhaul of the quantity and quality of education.

V

There can be no doubt that in early nineteenth-century England, the Churches as a whole were the most influential social institution in the country. To understand how they were influencing society and how they were influenced by it is then a necessary task of the economic, social and political historian. In this essay, we have seen that the Nonconformist churches were not the monolithic structure that such phrases as 'the nonconformist conscience' and 'English nonconformity' suggest. Rather, because of the theological explosion associated with Wesley, Whitefield, Edwards and Hall, and later the hardly less shattering impact of

[1] P. H. Wicksteed, *Memorials of the Rev. Charles Wicksteed* (London, 1886), p. 38.
[2] *Christian Reformer* (1844), pp. 280–1.
[3] *Memorials*, sup. cit., p. 39.

Priestley in one direction and the Transcendentalists in another, each of the major nonconformist sects found itself caught in a sociological scissors-grip. This necessarily implied adapting the social ethic naturally springing from the neo-theological insights in such a way as to minimize the centrifugal effect of issues which inevitably had class overtones. Hence we can see either direct contradiction or carefully studied ambivalence in many of the social pronouncements of leading Dissenters.

Certainly this is an oversimplification. It is not only true that the sociological tensions within the denominations effected the consistency and tenor of denominational pronouncements. It may be naïve to look for even the remotest degree of consistency or inspiration in the social pronouncement of ecclesiastics of any age and any sect. Equally, there is no reason to believe that the causation was uni-directional. It may be equally true that the multichromatic nature of denominational teaching affected the composition of each Church, so that each believer came to hear what he liked to believe. We may admit the force behind these methodological objections. But the evidence seems to suggest two important conclusions. First, except for repeal of the Corn Laws and the need for improved education, it is unhistorical to talk of undivided nonconformist allegiance to one single point of view on any of the leading social or economic questions of the day. From this follows the second major conclusion. Because they were inevitably divided on the great issues that called for social prophecy of the greatest quality, the nonconformist Churches gradually forfeited their right to be heard on such issues. It is not for nothing that the 'nonconformist conscience' of the late Victorian era is mainly associated with the relatively secondary issues of pubs and pimps, Sabbaths, betting and dancing. There is no one reason why the national influence of the Churches declined.[1] But it is surely incontestable, as Horace Mann declared in his Report in 1854,[2] that they forfeited much good-will by their failure to discharge their duties to society in the years of industrial revolution.

---

[1] We recognise, of course, the religious boom of the '70s and '80s, and the charismatic leadership of some of the great Nonconformists of those years. But we suggest that the influence of the great body of Nonconformity on national policies was not specially significant at this period.

[2] Horace Mann, *Sketches of the Religious Denominations of the Present Day* (London, 1854), pp. 94–5. But Mann maintained that there had been some improvement in the 'sympathy exhibited by professed Christians for the alleviation of their (working-class's) social burdens' by 1854.

8

R. M. HARTWELL

The Standard of Living Controversy:
A Summary

I

Much historical controversy is concerned with the propagation
of prejudice and the defence of doctrine, and it is in historical
controversy that we can see clearly that history is often a medium
for the advancement of doctrinaire theories about society. Most
historical controversies are rooted in contemporary problems and
debates; history is thus made relevant to the real world of the
historian. Indeed, it is the strong feeling that history is relevant that
makes appeal to 'the lessons of history' so universal. If history is no
longer seen, as it was in the nineteenth century, as the proper
training of men of affairs, it is nevertheless felt generally to be
relevant for the understanding of contemporary affairs. How contemporary, then, is the debate about the standard of living in
England during the industrial revolution? Certainly part of its
popularity is rooted in contemporary interests. The now vast
literature on economic growth has as one of its main themes the
effects of growth on living standards and way of life: the impact
of industrialization on the working classes is, therefore, a persistent theme of the literature of growth, as it has been of the
historians of the industrial revolution in England. It is for this
reason that comment on the standard of living controversy is
sometimes found far from the learned journals, as the following
two examples show.

In C. P. Snow's *The Two Cultures and the Scientific Revolution*
he comments about industrialization and about the industrial
revolution in England, arguing that 'industrialization is the only
hope of the poor'. 'To people like my grandfather', Snow wrote,
'there was no question that the industrial revolution was less bad
than what had gone before. The only question was how to make

it better.' In the widespread discussion which followed the publication in 1959 of Snow's lecture, much criticism was directed at
these statements. Snow was surprised, and replied: 'Did anyone
think that, in the primal terms in which I have just been discussing the poor countries of the present world, our ancestors'
conditions were so very different? Or that the industrial revolution
had not brought us in three or four generations to a state entirely
new in the harsh unrecorded continuity of poor men's lives?'
The expected economic dividend of modern economic growth,
Snow emphasizes, is an improved standard of living; he is sceptical,
therefore, that past economic growth, including the industrial
revolution in England, could have resulted in a deterioration in
living standards. 'No-one should feel it seriously possible', he
argued, 'to talk about a pre-industrial Eden, from which our
ancestors were, by the wicked machinations of applied science,
brutally expelled.'

A second example comes from a most unlikely source, the
1965–6 edition of R. Postgate's *Good Food Guide*, where, in the
Preface, the author makes a plea for this study of the history of
British food. 'British, or at any rate English, food was not
originally among the worst in the world', Postgate claims. 'On
the contrary, two centuries or less ago it was probably among the
best, if not the actual best.' Then, however, there was deterioration. 'English food—both the cooking and the raw material—
during the nineteenth century became not only infinitely worse
than French, but lower even than the modest standards in Germany, Italy and Spain. This was the result of two well-known
historical events whose effects it has been the policy of certain
recent historians to deny—the enclosure acts and the industrial
revolution. If you who read this have been affected by the special
pleading of writers like Professors Hayek and Ashton, I must ask
you to consult E. P. Thompson's *The Making of the English
Working Class*, for there is no room to argue here.' I am not
concerned with Postgate's claims about the history of English
food, for it would be foolish to take too seriously the economic
history embedded in an excellent guide to British eating houses.
I want, rather, to emphasize the intrusion of the standard-of-living
controversy into such a book, used relevantly to make a point
about alleged British eating habits over the last two centuries.

These two examples demonstrate how the debate about the

effect of English industrialization on the living standards of the poor has invaded contemporary discussion. It is important to emphasize, however, that the debate is not new and has been raging for a century and a half, beginning with the industrial revolution. Macaulay debated with Southey in the 1830s; Giffen with Toynbee in the 1880s; Clapham with the Hammonds in the 1920s; and Hartwell with Hobsbawm in the 1960s. Indeed, to get involved in this controversy is a life-long commitment. Involvement means notoriety, praise and abuse. For example, I have been praised as an anti-Marxist, although my intentions, and methods, are clearly non-ideological; and I have been attacked in a leading Soviet historical journal as a bourgeois reactionary. My supporters—whoever they might be—have been described in *The Times Literary Supplement* as 'immeasurably nastier' than the supporters of Dr Hobsbawm, nastier 'in their off-the-record comments in seminars and in their sniffs in the senior common rooms of Oxford'. The debate, then, has been long and bitter, but why the passion? Is such passion the inevitable result of the inconclusiveness of the long debate? The result of impatience rather than bad temper? Or is it the result of strongly-held and deeply-felt views about the character of social and economic change?

Let me make two points. First, it is not the protraction of this debate which has sharpened tempers. No exchange was sharper than that between Macaulay and Southey right at the beginning of the argument. Second, in spite of the considerable historical efforts of many exponents of that semi-exact social science, economic history, the controversy still rages. The contesters will not give up. What then has the controversy proved? Is it that it concerns a problem so complex that it is impossible to solve, or is it because the evidence is so confusing and incomplete that it does not provide a firm basis for a solution? The controversy surely proves that when historical events are complex and large, when evidence is plentiful but confusing, when feelings and beliefs are affected, then differences between historians tend to be lively and, often, not resolvable. In the case of the standard-of-living controversy the modern debate has been further enlivened by two special factors: belief in doctrine that industrialization in England proceeded *in a certain way* (as expounded by Marx); concern for the underdeveloped countries of the world. The Marxists declare allegiance to a particular interpretation of the industrial revolution, and are more concerned with doctrinal orthodoxy than with historical truth. The students of underdevelopment are concerned with the effects of the industrialization of an economy on the peoples of that economy. Both concerns centre on one question. What are the rewards and costs for the working classes of economic growth through industrialization? It is interest in this question—on growth and welfare—which makes the debate about living standards during the industrial revolution a public debate rather than a controversy solely among economic historians.

II

The expected dividend of industrialization today is an increasing standard of living and a changed way of life. In terms of total welfare, the net result is difficult if not impossible to measure, and hence to evaluate. The less tangible factor, incapable of exact measurement, is the value attached to a way of life, because this involves a consideration of wants not normally valued in the market place. Industrialization means, inevitably, a great change in the social and cultural environment, as well as in the economic environment. A final calculation of welfare must compare different ways of life, and this calculation calls for skills and knowledge beyond those of either historian or economist. However, the historian can answer two questions about the industrial revolution in England: whether or not the worker's 'bundle of goods' increased; whether or not the worker willingly gave up a rural, pre-industrial way of life for the way of life of an urban industrial society. Perhaps the latter question is the more important, for it provides convincing evidence about what the workers wanted. And, as C. P. Snow has noted, 'with singular unanimity, in any country where they have had the chance, the poor have walked off the land into the factories as fast as the factories could take them'. In the case of England, evidence of wage differentials and labour migration strongly suggest both that living standards improved and also that workers welcomed the changed way of life. Regional wage variations, as E. W. Gilboy has demonstrated, were considerable in the eighteenth century, and the areas of higher wages were the industrializing areas, the areas of immigration, and where there was 'an ambitious and active working class'. 'The expanding industrial centres were constantly drawing labour from the surrounding country'. In spite of such evidence, however, the debate continues. Why?

As I suggested above, historical controversy stems from the prejudices of the historian and from the complexity of the historical event being debated. In the case of the industrial revolution, the controversy about living standards has also been bedevilled by confusion: the historians, with unprofessional obstinacy, or with deliberate obfuscation, have refused to make clear what they have been arguing about. There have been four main types of confusion: sometimes historians have been talking about the standard of living, sometimes about the way of life; there has also been a failure to define *whose* standard of living was being discussed—that of all workers, or of industrial workers (excluding agricultural workers), or of artisans (excluding labourers), etc.; another confusion has arisen, partly because of the way in which official statistics have been collected, because it has not always been clear what geographical area was being considered—Great Britain, or England, etc., when obviously the inclusion of Ireland in this period would have depressed all income averages: and, finally, there have been doubts about the time periods being compared—1750 to 1850, 1760 to 1830, 1800 to 1840, 1800 to 1850, etc. When such confusions were intensified by the political and social bias of the historian, it is not difficult to see why differences of interpretation have been compounded into irreconcilable points of view.

From the beginning the debate about the social and economic consequences of the industrial revolution has been, plainly, a political debate: the Tory Southey versus the Whig Macaulay about the virtues of pre-industrial mercantilist-aristocratic as against industrial laissez-faire society (Macaulay's essay on Southey being a brilliant and vigorous defence of laissez-faire); the Marxist Hobsbawm versus the Liberal Ashton about whether or not Marx's interpretation of the industrial revolution was correct (Ashton, like Macaulay, taking a Whig-Liberal interpretation of English history). The debate has also been methodological, between those like Clapham who believed in quantification, where it was possible and relevant, and those like the Hammonds who believed that the quantification of social events was misleading. Certainly quantification now threatens, or seems to threaten, a profession more skilled in writing than in counting, but the fear and distrust of the statistical historian is also profoundly humanist in inspiration; there is real concern that by counting only what can be counted whole areas of human enterprise will be relegated to the unknown and unknowable.

As well as by confusion and by political and methodological passion, the historian of the industrial revolution is likely to be misled by the peculiar quality of his main evidence. The complexity and diversity of source material for this period is great,but the most accessible, the largest and the most used source, the Parliamentary Papers, is concerned mainly with the ills and seldom with the goods of industrializing society. Its massive evidence was aimed at legislation, not at the historian; a parliamentary inquiry was part of an orderly sequence of the identification of a social ill, agitation for inquiry and remedy, detailed Parliamentary inquiry, legislative action, and, finally, inspection. Generally, the great Parliamentary inquiries were part of the process of identifying, analysing and remedying social ills, and for this reason, their evidence was not necessarily typical of society or economy. However, they have been used too uncritically by the historians. On the other hand, the records of particular industrial firms, in which continuous and firm data about wages can be found, have not been used so extensively, except by the Manchester historians (Unwin, Daniels and Ashton, for example) whose conclusions about living standards during the industrial revolution differed so markedly from those who, like the Hammonds, depended almost exclusively on Parliamentary inquiries and the Public Records Office.

The result of all this has been two histories of the industrial revolution, labelled *pessimist* and *optimist* by E. J. Hobsbawm. As T. E. Gregory wrote long ago: 'The England of Toynbee and the Hammonds is not the England of Tooke and Newmarch'. To bring the debate forward: the England of Hobsbawm and Thompson is not the England of Ashton and Hartwell. Rather than call these differing interpretations *pessimist* and *optimist*, I would prefer to call them *catastrophic* and *growth* theories of the industrial revolution. In this I am supported by E. P. Thompson who writes of 'the classic catastrophic orthodoxy'. The catastrophic theory pictures the destruction of a valued way of life and its replacement by an inferior and degraded way of life, along with a deterioration in the standard of living; the growth theory sees the industrial revolution as economic growth through industrialization, with the replacement of an urban for a rural way of life, with the growing independence of the working classes, and with a gradual but sustained improvement in the standard of living for the masses.

III

Before surveying the evidence about living standards during the industrial revolution, we can begin with the assumption that there is no disagreement between the controversialists that the period of industrialization was one of sustained growth of output, a period during which real national product grew faster and over a longer period than ever before in history, even though there were cyclical set-backs. This growth was admitted in the 1920s by the Hammonds, and more recently by E. J. Hobsbawm and E. P. Thompson. Given this growth, however, in order to prove the catastrophic theory of the industrial revolution, it is necessary to devise a model of the English economy of the period, which will fit the facts of history, but in which there was sustained growth of output over a long period of time without raising general living standards. The exponents of catastrophe, however, have not thought of the historical problem explicitly as that of explaining how a particular example of sustained growth, the industrial revolution, resulted in falling living standards over a long period, when the expectations of common sense, economic theory and later examples of growth suggest the opposite. Nevertheless, three models of growth plus immiseration can be found in the writings of the catastrophic school. The first is the *Malthusian Trap Model*, in which gross national product grows but population grows faster so that productivity is outstripped by population growth. For example, S. Pollard has written that in the period up to 1800, 'in a country where there was no wide and fertile spaces left for settlement, and at a time when foreign trade in foodstuffs was no more than marginal, [population growth] was bound to lead to a race between the additional mouths to be fed, and the ability of home agriculture to feed them'. He concludes that there was a 'temporary failure of the English food supply, which lasted from 1770 to 1800', which was basically due to 'the marked increase in population'. E. P. Thompson also has remarked on 'the exceptional stresses resulting from the population explosion'. This is, of course, undiluted Malthus, but nonetheless the model is a realistic one: the example of Ireland in the century after 1750 is a good example of a country in which population increased faster than output, culminating in the catastrophe of the Famine.

The second model is the *Biased Income Distribution Model*, in which income distribution during economic growth is so biased against the worker that it not only deprives him of any of the increases in product, but it actually reduces his absolute share of an increasing product. And so the rich get richer and the poor get poorer. Ever since Engels examined the English poor in 1844, biased distribution has been the main argument used by those who believed, like Engels, that living standards deteriorated with industrialization. The model now takes two forms: the exploitation model and the forced savings model. The exploitation model is the traditional model, used by Engels, Marx, Toynbee, the Fabians, the Hammonds, and recently by Thompson and Hobsbawm. As E. P. Thompson has written, the industrial revolution was a period of 'more intensive and more transparent forms of economic exploitation'. 'For most working people', he concludes, 'the crucial experience of the Industrial Revolution was felt in terms of changes in the nature and intensity of exploitation'. This exploitation was achieved by expropriation of product in the forms of rent, interest and profits; it is seen by the pessimistic historian as deliberate and malicious, the strong greedily and inhumanely robbing the weak, the rich living on the efforts of the poor. Insofar as exploitation is put in the form of a model it is a simple one, a productive process in which the capitalist-employer has all the power and the worker-employee has nothing to sell but his labour and has no bargaining power. The forced-savings model is a recent innovation, stemming directly from economists' theories of growth. Simply stated it is this: during the process of growth, indeed causing growth, there is a large diversion of income from consumption to capital formation, thus reducing real incomes. This analysis for the industrial revolution has been popularized in particular by E. J. Hamilton and S. Pollard. Hamilton claims that the industrial revolution was achieved during a period of profit inflation, when prices rose faster than wages; Pollard argues that there was a 'unique pressure on resources' during the industrial revolution, and a need 'for a critical period' of 'the greatest amount of output and the lowest level of personal consumption which could be imposed on the population'. Such arguments have been seized on eagerly by the catastrophic school. As E. P. Thompson has written: 'Britain in the industrial revolution was encountering the problems of "take-off"; heavy long-term investment—canals, mills, railways, foundries, mines, utilities—was at the expense of current consumption; the generations of workers between 1790 and 1840 sacrificed some, or all, of their prospects of increased consumption to the future'.

The third model is the *Deteriorating Terms of Trade Model*, in which the terms of trade of a trading economy during its growth are so unfavourable that continually increasing exports are needed to pay for a decreasing flow of essential imports. In applying this model to industrial revolution England, A. J. Taylor and S. Pollard have argued that much of the benefit of England's industrialization was exported. As Pollard says: 'Since the terms of trade worsened, part of the increased output was "lost" in conversion to consumption goods by foreign trade'.

These, then, are the models of immiserizing growth which have been suggested by the exponents of 'the classic catastrophic orthodoxy'. But are such models reconcilable with the facts of history? First, let me make two general points: the time period for the testing of these models is a long one, from 50 to 100 years, so that the conditions which produced the alleged decline in living standards must have persisted over a long period; empirical studies of modern growth, in many countries, for example by S. Kuznets, show that over a long period of growth there has been generally the simultaneous rise of gross national product, capital accumulation and real incomes for the masses. Turning to the realities of the English economy during the industrial revolution, it is possible to show that the suggested models do not conform with history.

As regards the *Malthusian Trap Model*, the aggregate series that have been compiled, both for national income and industrial output, show rates of growth faster than the rate of growth of population. Certainly the figures are not so convincing that they can be accepted unquestioningly; but no aggregate figures to prove that output grew slower than population have been devised, or even suggested. It would seem, therefore, that *average per capita real income* rose during the industrial revolution. As regards the *Biased Income Distribution Model*, there is no convincing evidence of a change in distribution, through exploitation or forced savings, that would have reduced absolutely the real incomes of the working classes. On the contrary, over the period the government intervened increasingly in social and economic life to correct income inequality, as also did a host of humanitarian and charitable organizations bent on alleviating the sufferings of the poor. In any case, income distribution could have been biased against the worker increasingly, and their real incomes could still have risen if the rate of growth of output had been sufficiently great; and during the great war against France, this is probably what happened. Perhaps the two distributive mechanisms of unemployment and inflation could have caused serious losses of income for the working classes, and downgraded their living standards? As regards unemployment the evidence of its incidence (because of the trade cycle, or structural and technological change) does not reveal losses which more than offset the gains of those in employment. On the contrary, the cycle hardly dented the secular rise in national product, and the employment opportunities of new or growing industries more than offset the loss of employment from structural or technical change. For example, cotton factories created much more employment than the unemployment they also created by making hand-loom weavers redundant; similarly the railways demanded massive employment which dwarfed the unemployment caused by the competition with roads and canals. Inflation, with money wages lagging behind prices, certainly held back real wages during the war, but after 1815, when prices were falling and money wages remained constant or rose, real wages were rising, in spite of an alleged surplus of labour and in spite of weak organized bargaining by labour. This post-war relationship between wages and prices in a period of weakly organized labour is the most awkward single phenomenon to be explained away by the catastrophic school.

If inflation did not deprive the worker of the fruits of economic growth, what of capital accumulation? Was the need to refrain from consumption so great that living standards fell? It is not difficult to show, however, that better rather than more capital (more proportionately to national income) increased productivity in England during the industrial revolution. Better capital took the forms of better equipment, better organization and management, and better human capital (more skilled workers and more efficient managers); it was technical, organizational and human progress rather than any dramatic increase in fixed capital proportions which increased productivity during the industrial revolution. Capital formation, as a percentage of national income, probably did not reach ten per cent until the 1840s, when there was a massive building of railways and a marked increase in the size of industrial units. Indeed the rate of capital formation was so low during the industrial revolution that it almost certainly explains some of the distress of the period—a point seldom noted by the pessimists; for example, the failure to devote enough resources to the social infrastructure, particularly in the rapidly growing cities, was the cause of considerable suffering. It should be remembered, moreover, that investment in capital goods was made in the expectation of increasing productivity, at least in the next period; over the 50 to 100 years of the industrial revolution— a very long period—if capital accumulation did not increase productivity, with a large increase in output and incomes, it must have been largely unproductive, which it patently was not. There is no evidence, except during the war, that investment was anything but highly productive with consequential effects on employment and incomes.

There is, finally, the *Deteriorating Terms of Trade Model*. But there is no evidence that the terms of trade were so perversely unfavourable as to result in immiserizing growth. Certainly the terms of trade were unfavourable after 1815, and, because of this, some of the benefits of the industrial revolution were exported, but the reduced price of manufactured goods, at home as well as abroad, benefited the English worker, as did the increased international trade which cheaper exports stimulated.

It seems, therefore, that none of the suggested immiseration models fit the facts of history. On the contrary, the historical facts were: average per capita real income increased; there was no trend in distribution against the workers; the terms of trade were not so unfavourable as to seriously affect living standards; after 1815 prices fell more than money wages; per capita consumption of food and other consumer goods increased; capital accumulation did not make excessive demands on total income; government increasingly intervened to protect and raise the living standards of the poor. To these facts should be added evidence about population. Population was rising rapidly after 1780, the result almost certainly of a rising birth rate and, more important, of a falling death rate, the consequence not of improved medicine but of environmental and nutritional improvements. As living standards rose with industrialization parents had more children and more survived. The facts of history also conform with the expectations of economic theory: economic growth over a long period should result in increased living standards for the mass of the people. And the industrial revolution in England is an example of long-term economic growth. But, it must be emphasized, living standards were neither high nor rising fast for most workers. Poverty, often desperate poverty, was to remain the lot of many of the workers of England until the mid-twentieth century. To prove that the standard of living had improved is to prove neither that it was adequate in any objective sense, nor that the new industrial society was without social and economic ills. The question at issue has been the trend—whether or not the trend in living standards was up or down—and about this there is little doubt: the standard of living was rising.

IV

Is the controversy over? As regards the standard of living—the bundle of goods—it should be, and, indeed, appears to be. Even E. P. Thompson, the most convinced pessimist, now agrees that 'no serious scholar is willing to argue that everything got worse' and that, on the contrary, there was 'over the period 1790–1840 . . . a slight improvement in average material standards'. However, Mr Thompson also argues, that 'over the same period there was intensified exploitation, greater insecurity, and increasing human misery. By 1840 most people were 'better off' than their fore-runners had been 50 years before, but they had suffered and continued to suffer this slight improvement as a catastrophic experience'. Mr Thompson also argues that 'it is possible for statistical averages and human experience to run in opposite directions', and that 'people may consume more goods and become less happy or less free at the same time', and that 'the process of industrialization must, in any conceivable social context, entail suffering and the destruction of older and valued ways of life'. I quote Mr Thompson at some length because no-one since the Hammonds has written with such sympathy and passion about the working classes of England, and no-one illustrates more clearly how the catastrophic school has changed the field of dispute, from the standard of living to the way of life, from the bundle of goods to less measurable phenomena like exploitation, misery and freedom. The catastrophic school believes that, whatever happened to the standard of living, the way of life changed for the worse.

However, although living standards were still desperately low, and although the working classes were still largely excluded from social and political power, it was during the industrial revolution that they began to exercise effective and sustained control over their own lives, and to have sustained political and industrial power, for the first time in history. Certainly the thesis that the way of life worsened during the industrial revolution should be investigated as thoroughly as the thesis that the standard of living worsened. Unfortunately a way of life cannot be summed up neatly as a quantifiable bundle of goods; changes in a way of life are probably impossible to measure and certainly difficult to evaluate. On the quality of a social environment, prejudice rather than science too often dictates the views of the historian. There are neither adequate tools nor sufficient research to decide conclusively about the way of life in England during the industrial revolution. Only when the historian has delved deeper into the archives, and only when the social scientists have developed a methodology of social history, will there be a solution to this long-standing and fascinating debate to which I have devoted so much arduous yet pleasurable effort.